Divine

Transformation

If not now, when?

Do not copy the behavior and customs of this world,

but let God transform you into a new person by

changing the way you think. Then you will learn

to know God's will for you, which is

good and pleasing and perfect.

Romans 12:2 NLT

Dr. Rachel Comeaux

Foreword By Kevin Zadai, PhD

Cover Design by Jennifer M. Beslin

Cover Art by Gabrielle E. Comeaux

Cover Collaboration Alexis A. McClarty

Please note that the author's publishing style capitalizes certain pronouns in Scripture that refer to the Father, Son, and Holy Spirit, which may differ from some publishers' styles. Take note that the name "satan" and related names are not capitalized. We choose not to acknowledge him, even to the point of violating accepted grammatical rules.
Cover art by Gabrielle Comeaux, Cover design by Jennifer Beslin, Foreword by Kevin Zadai, PhD

For more information, follow me on Facebook:
https://www.facebook.com/rachelacomeaux

Contents

Foreword

by Dr. Kevin Zadai, President of Warrior Notes School of Ministry

It is a joy and an honor to introduce this powerful book, Divine Transformation. Whenever the Lord works to accelerate His people into their purpose, He releases revelation that brings clarity, identity, and supernatural change. As we read through these chapters, we receive that same impartation—an invitation from Heaven for believers to rise above the limitations of this world and walk in the fullness of what Jesus purchased for them.

Transformation is not a concept; it is a spiritual reality made available through the Holy Spirit. The Kingdom of God operates by revelation, and revelation produces change at the deepest level. This book is filled with that kind of revelation—truth that renews the mind, anchors the heart, and positions God's people to step into their destiny with boldness. You will not only read about transformation; you will experience the invitation to live it.

One of the greatest truths I have learned from my encounters with Jesus is that Heaven is always calling us upward. You were never designed to live from your past, from your wounds, or from the limitations of natural thinking. You were created to live from the glory of God. The Holy Spirit is constantly working to unveil your true identity, align you with God's original intention, and empower you to walk in supernatural victory. This book echoes that divine agenda and provides practical biblical wisdom that will help you cooperate with the Spirit's work in your life.

As you journey through these pages, you will discover key principles about surrender, identity, acceleration, and the reality of God's presence. These truths are not theories—they are spiritual laws. When applied, they produce fruit. When believed, they unlock freedom. When acted upon, they propel you into God's plan at a supernatural pace. Heaven responds to hunger, and I believe this book will stir your hunger for more of Jesus.

I encourage you to read Divine Transformation with an open heart. Let the Holy Spirit speak to you. Let Him highlight areas where He is inviting you to grow. Let Him reveal the parts of your identity that have been hidden beneath fear, trauma, or discouragement. You may be surprised at how much Heaven has been waiting for your "yes." God never forces transformation—He partners with yielded vessels. If you will simply agree with Him, He will do more in a moment than you could accomplish in a lifetime.

My prayer is that the insights in this book will activate a new level of confidence in your walk with God. May your spiritual eyes be opened. May your heart be strengthened. May the fire of the Holy Spirit bring clarity, healing, and acceleration. And may you come to know, with absolute certainty, that you were created for destiny.

Heaven has a plan for you. The Holy Spirit is your Helper. Jesus is your victory.

Now step into your divine transformation.

—Dr. Kevin Zadai

President, Warrior Notes School of Ministry

Introduction

Now all discipline seems to be painful at the time, yet later it will

produce a transformation of character, bringing a harvest of

righteousness and peace to those who yield to it.

Hebrews 12:11 TPT

I thank the Lord Jesus and give Him all the glory and honor for everything. He has transformed me in every area of my life. I will share many treasured revelations that the Lord has revealed to me thus far. If you are seeking divine transformation in your life, this book is for you. Join me now on this journey of discovering divine transformation by the power of the Holy Spirit. With God all things are possible.

1

Are You Ready for a Change?

satan, who is the god of this world, has blinded the minds of those

who don't believe. They are unable to see the glorious light of

the Good News. They don't understand this message about the

glory of Christ, who is the exact likeness of God.

II Corinthians 4:4 NLT

Ask yourself these questions: Are you ready for a change? If not now, when? When will it ever be the right time or circumstance? What's been holding you back? What's hindering you? Is it trauma, rejection, addiction, fear, anxiety, offense, or unforgiveness? Are you scared of change? The world around us is dark and chaotic right now. Do you feel like you are being tossed to and fro, not knowing which way to go at times? Are you busy and distracted? Are you struggling to discern the truth from the lies? Do you feel like you are in a small, dark place? Are you defeated because you believe the lies from the enemy? Well, the god of this world, satan, has blinded the minds of those who do not believe in Christ. He does not want you to know the truth. He does not even want you to think he exists. He likes to deceive and hide or cloak himself. Do you want to come out of the darkness? You do not have to stay there. There is a way out!

When God called me to Himself, I recall having these thoughts. The one that stands out the most is 'If not now, when?' When will I quit smoking and drinking? When will I stop living in sin? How do I stop? I have tried so many times on my own, and I failed miserably. Quitting is something I did when things snowballed and got too hard. The devil was attacking me to keep me in a small, defeated place so I would not fulfill my God-given destiny. I helped him, even though I did not realize it, because of the poor choices I was making.

Once you were dead because of your disobedience and your many sins. You used to live in sin, just like the rest of the world, obeying the devil—the commander of the powers in the unseen world. He is the spirit at work in the hearts of those who refuse to obey God. All of us used to live that way, following the passionate desires and inclinations of our sinful nature. By our very nature, we were subject to God's anger, just like everyone else. But God is so rich in mercy, and he loved us so much, that even though we were dead because of our sins, he gave us life when he raised Christ from the dead.

(It is only by God's grace that you have been saved!)

Ephesians 2:1-5 NLT

The Bible says here that before I received Christ, I used to obey the devil and live a sinful life. Have you received Christ? Our choices matter. We are presented with many choices every day. You may think, How can my choices matter to others? What I choose only affects me, but this is false. We are all connected and our choices matter. If we are in Christ, we are His body, and he is the head of us all. It is like the little toe. You may not think it matters but if you bump it, you will feel it. No one is too small or insignificant. It is just the opposite in the kingdom of Heaven. The Bible says the least in the Kingdom is the greatest. God wrote a book about you before you were born.

You saw me before I was born. Every day of my life was recorded in your book. Every moment was laid out before a single day had passed.

Psalms 139:16 NLT

The God of the universe wrote a book about every one of us before we were born. How awesome is that! Our books are written as if we will all go to Heaven. God gives us a choice. We can choose Him and choose life, or we can choose death. We can choose blessings or curses. God does not want anyone to go to Hell. Hell was not created for man but for the devil and demons.

Do you want to experience and walk in peace every day? This is attainable. Jesus gave us a gift of supernatural peace. It is not peace as the world gives. Jesus's peace is real, tangible, and powerful.

"I am leaving you with a gift—peace of mind and heart. And the peace I give is a gift the world cannot give. So don't be troubled or afraid."

John 14:27 NLT

Father God, I pray that the Lord will reveal the truth to you according to the Word of God. I pray for you to experience God as you read this book. I pray that what Paul wrote in Ephesians will be over you now in Jesus' name.

[I always pray] that the God of our Lord Jesus Christ, the Father of glory, may grant you a spirit of wisdom and of revelation [that gives you a deep and personal and intimate insight] into the true knowledge of Him [for we know the Father through the Son]. And [I pray] that the eyes of your heart [the very center and core of your being] may be enlightened [flooded with light by the Holy Spirit], so that you will know and cherish the hope [the divine guarantee, the confident expectation] to which He has called you, the riches of His glorious inheritance in the saints (God's people), and [so that you will begin to know] what the immeasurable and unlimited and surpassing greatness of His [active, spiritual] power is in us who believe. These are in accordance with the working of His mighty strength which He produced in Christ when He raised Him from the dead and seated Him at His own right hand in the heavenly places, far above all rule, and authority, and power, and dominion [whether angelic or human], and [far above] every name that is named [above every title that can be conferred], not only in this age and world but also in the one to come. And He put all things [in every realm] in subjection under Christ's feet, and [j]appointed Him as [supreme and authoritative] head over all

things in the church, which is His body, the fullness of Him who fills
and completes all things in all [believers].

Ephesians 1:17-23 AMP

Jesus said, "that whoever believes in Him should not perish
but have eternal life. For God so loved the world that He gave His
only begotten Son, that whoever believes in Him should not perish
but have everlasting life. For God did not send His Son into the

world to condemn the world, but that the world through Him
might be saved."

John 3:15-17 NKJV

Salvation is a free gift from God. All we need to do is accept this gift by believing in Jesus. The Good News is Jesus came to redeem us and give us everlasting life. It is our choice to receive it. God gave each of us free will so we could choose Him. We have the power to choose between life and death. God wanted a family, not puppets, so He gave us free will. He loved us so much that He sent His only begotten Son to die on the cross for the sins of the world so we can have eternal life with Him. God does not want anyone to perish, but for everyone to have eternal life. Jesus said, "Eternal life means to know and experience You, Father God, as the only true God and to know and experience Jesus Christ, as the Son whom You have sent." (John 17:3 TPT)

But whenever someone turns to the Lord, the veil is taken away. For the Lord is the Spirit, and wherever the Spirit of the Lord is, there is freedom. So all of us who have had that veil removed can see and reflect the glory of the Lord. And the Lord—who is the Spirit—makes us more and more like him as we are changed into his glorious image.

2 Corinthians 3:16-18 NLT

The word divine in Webster's 1828 dictionary is defined as pertaining to the true God; as the divine nature; divine perfections. 3. Partaking of the nature of God 5. Godlike; heavenly; excellent in the highest degree; extraordinary; apparently above what is human.

The word transformation in Webster's 1828 dictionary is defined as the act or operation of changing the form or external appearance. 2. Transmutation; the change of one metal into another, as of copper or tin into gold. 3. The change of the soul into a divine substance. 5. In theology, a change of heart in man, by which his disposition and temper are conformed to the divine image; a change from enmity to holiness and love.

The word "change" in Webster's 1828 dictionary is defined as: 1. To cause to turn or pass from one state to another; to alter, or make different; to vary in external form, or in essence; to change the color or shape of a thing; to change the countenance; to change the heart or life.

When you receive the Lord in your heart, your face changes! You literally are transformed into a new species. Your spirit is born again and is saved. You carry the Lord, and the joy and glory shines through your face. The more you surrender yourself to the Lord, the more freedom you have, and your face will shine brighter with the glory of the Lord! Amen! Hallelujah!

I thank you, Lord, that you are our constant and you change not. Please help us to seek your face and change for the better. When we believe, live, and apply true biblical principles in the word of God, our whole world changes for the better. If you change your words, you will change your life.

So, let's put these two words together. Divine transformation (God Change) occurs in a person who partakes in the nature of the true God, undergoing a change in their heart that conforms their character to the divine image, transforming them from being an enemy of God to one of holiness and love. Our true reality and

15

identity will emerge when we believe in Christ, and the veil is lifted. A whole new realm will open up to you as you seek after God. When you said, "Seek my face," my heart said to you, "Your face, Lord, I will seek." (Psalms 27:8 NKJV) You will be changed and turn from darkness to light in every area that you submit to the Lord. You are changed into the image of God as you move from glory to glory or from revelation to revelation. Divine transformation is supernatural. You cannot do it in your own strength, but by spending time with the supernatural One True Living God, you are divinely changed. You become what you behold, so if you seek after the Lord, you will become like Him. The Holy Spirit will guide and instruct you in many ways throughout this exciting supernatural journey.

Jesus explained, "I am the Way, I am the Truth, and I am the Life. No one comes next to the Father except through union with me. To know me is to know my Father too.

John 14:6 TPT

Our God, our Creator, is three in one: Father God, Jesus, and the Holy Spirit. Jesus is the only way to the Father, as we see here in John 14:6. When we choose Jesus, we become a new creature in Christ! The old man is dead, and behold, all things become new. (2

Cor 5:17) Then we must turn and follow Jesus and become His disciple. We must do the work and get trained up in the things of the Lord. The Holy Spirit will lead you into all TRUTH. (John 16)

Jesus replied, "I assure you, no one can enter the Kingdom of God without being born of water and the Spirit."

John 3:5 NLT

The book of Romans shows us the way to salvation because we have all sinned and fallen short of the glory of God. The wages of sin is death, and eternal life in Christ Jesus our Lord is a gift from God. If you confess with your mouth that Jesus is Lord and believe in your heart that God raised Him from the dead, you shall be saved.

For everyone has sinned; we all fall short of God's glorious standard.

Romans 3:23 NLT

For the wages of sin is death, but the free gift of God is eternal life through Christ Jesus our Lord.

Romans 6:23 NLT

If you openly declare that Jesus is Lord and believe in your heart that God raised him from the dead, you will be saved.

Romans 10:9 NLT

So, Jesus told them this story: "If a man has a hundred sheep and one of them gets lost, what will he do? Won't he leave the ninety-nine others in the wilderness and go to search for the one that is lost until he finds it? And when he has found it, he will joyfully carry it home on his shoulders. When he arrives, he will call together his friends and neighbors, saying, 'Rejoice with me because I have found my lost sheep.' In the same way, there is more joy in heaven over one lost sinner who repents and returns to God than over ninety-nine others who are righteous and haven't strayed away!

Luke 15:3-7 NLT

Jesus is calling your name. You are His precious lost sheep. Are you ready to break the negative patterns in your life? One choice today can change the trajectory of your whole life. You are not too far gone. There is nothing so terrible that you have done that the Lord will not forgive you for. God is merciful and forgiving. He loves us so much that He sent His Son, Jesus, to die on the cross for us and redeem us. Will you answer the call of salvation today and receive Jesus as your Lord and Savior? Now is the time! Today is your day!

Are you ready to begin your divine transformation? If not now, when? You can go to Heaven! Pray with me now to receive Jesus and start the divine transformation you are seeking.

Father God,

I confess that I am a sinner. I confess that I need Your Son, Jesus. Please forgive me for all sins known and unknown. Lord Jesus, I believe You came in the flesh, died for me, and that You are alive and listening to me now. I now turn from all of my sins and welcome You into my heart. Come and take control of my life. Make me the kind of person You want me to be. Now, fill me with Your Holy Spirit and fire. The Holy Spirit will teach me how to live for You. I acknowledge and confess You before men as my Savior and my Lord. In Jesus' name, Amen.

Praise Jesus! Welcome to the Kingdom of Heaven. You are now born again of the Spirit of God, and all of Heaven is rejoicing because you decided to follow Jesus. Jesus said He would not leave us orphans; our Father God would send another one like Him to us. God sent us the Holy Spirit. The Holy Spirit is the Spirit of Truth. God has now come to make His home in you. Keeping the Lord's commandments shows Him you love Him, and He will love you and manifest Himself to you.

2

Divine Intervention

Jesus Prophesies about the Holy Spirit

"Loving me empowers you to obey my commands. And I will ask the Father, and he will give you another Savior, the Holy Spirit of Truth, who will be to you a friend just like me—and he will never leave you. The world won't receive him because they can't see him or know him. But you know him intimately because he remains with you and will live inside you. "I promise that I will never leave you helpless or abandon you as orphans—I will come back to you! Soon I will leave this world, and they will see me no longer, but you will see me, because I will live again, and you will come alive too. So when that day comes, you will know that I am living in the

Father and that you are one with me, for I will be living in you. Those who truly love me are those who obey my commands. Whoever passionately loves me will be passionately loved by my Father. And I will passionately love him in return and will reveal myself to him." Then one of the disciples named Judas (not Judas Iscariot) said, "Lord, why is it you will only reveal your identity to us and not to everyone?" Jesus replied, "Loving me empowers you to obey my word. And my Father will love you so deeply that we will come to you and make you our dwelling place. But those who don't love me will not obey my words. The Father did not send me to speak my own revelation, but the words of my Father. I am telling you this while I am still with you. But when the Father sends the Spirit of Holiness, the One like me who sets you free, he will teach you all things in my name. And he will inspire you to remember every word that I've told you. (Footnote: The Aramaic is translated as "the Redeemer from the curse.") "I leave the gift of peace with you—my peace. Not the kind of fragile peace given by the world, but my perfect peace. Don't yield to fear or be troubled in your hearts—instead, be courageous! "Remember what I've told you, that I must go away, but I promise to come back to you. So, if you truly love me, you will be glad for me, since I'm returning to my Father, who is greater than I. So when all of these things happen, you will still trust and cling to me. I won't speak with you much longer, for the ruler of this dark world is coming. But he has no power over me, for he has nothing to use against me. I am doing exactly what the Father destined for me to accomplish, so that the world will discover how much I love my Father. Now come with me."

John 14:15-31 TPT

Are you ready for divine intervention? If not now, when? There is more of God to discover! We must be rooted and grounded in the Word of God. The Holy Spirit will reveal His Word to you by His Spirit. The revelations will literally become a part of you. No one will be able to take the revelations or the freedom you gain from them away from you. Hallelujah!

Who is the Holy Spirit? In John 14:26 AMPC, it says, "But the Comforter (Counselor, Helper, Intercessor, Advocate, Strengthener, Standby), the Holy Spirit, Whom the Father will send in My name [in My place, to represent Me and act on My behalf], He will teach you all things. And He will cause you to recall (will remind you of, bring to your remembrance) everything I have told you."

This scripture is so profound that our Father God cares so much for us that He sent the Holy Spirit to help, guide, defend, comfort, console us, and so much more. The Holy Spirit is the Redeemer who ends the curse in our lives. He enforces the blessings of God in our lives! Hallelujah!

But the one who joins himself to the Lord is mingled into one spirit with him. Have you forgotten that your body is now the sacred temple of the Spirit of Holiness, who lives in you? You do not belong to yourself any longer, for the gift of God, the Holy Spirit, lives inside your sanctuary. You were God's expensive purchase, paid for with

tears of blood, so by all means, then, use your body to bring glory to God!

1 Corinthians 6:17, 19-20 TPT

We are entwined with God, and we are the temple of the Holy Spirit. We were purchased with the Blood of Jesus. We are one with Him, and we should live each day to bring Him glory. Amen!

"From now on, worshiping the Father will not be a matter of the right place but with a right heart. For God is a Spirit, and he longs to have sincere worshipers who adore him in the realm of the Spirit and in truth."

John 4:23-24 TPT

We must have the Spirit of God to worship Him in spirit and truth. God is seeking true worshippers. People who love Him and lay down their lives to allow God to live through them entirely. Allow the Lord to occupy every place inside of your soul. True freedom and worship are beautiful to God.

Just before he ascended into heaven, Jesus left instructions through the Holy Spirit for the apostles he had chosen. After the sufferings of his cross, Jesus appeared alive many times to these same apostles over a forty-day period, proving to them with many convincing signs that he had been resurrected. During these encounters, he taught them the truths of God's kingdom. Jesus instructed them, "Do not leave Jerusalem, but wait here until you receive the gift I told you about, the gift the Father has promised. For John baptized you in water, but in a few days from now you will be baptized in the Holy Spirit!"

Acts 1:2-5 TPT

The Holy Spirit was sent to the church in the upper room on the day of Pentecost, and they were all baptized and spoke in other languages as the Holy Spirit gave them utterance.

The Holy Spirit is holy. Holy means exalted or worthy of complete devotion as one perfect in goodness and righteousness; dedicated, consecrated to God, sacred, morally, and spiritually excellent. God makes us holy.

The Holy Spirit is our advocate. An Attorney is an advocate. An advocate is one who defends or maintains a cause or proposal; one who supports or promotes the interests of a cause or group. The Holy Spirit is the attorney on your case.

The Holy Spirit is our comforter. A comforter is a person or thing that provides consolation. The Holy Spirit can wrap you up like a warm blanket.

The Holy Spirit is our counselor. A counselor is a person who gives advice or counseling, a lawyer, specifically one who provides advice in law and manages cases for clients in court, or a confidential advisor. He cares about every detail. The Holy Spirit wants to get to the root of the problem. Free counseling! So, talk to him about everything.

The Holy Spirit is our strengthener. A strengthener gives or adds strength.

The Holy Spirit is our teacher. The Bible says He leads us into all truth. He corrects us by giving us the truth. Truth also means reality. We need to accept the reality that the Holy Spirit reveals to us to grow and mature.

The Holy Spirit is our standby. Standby means someone ready for duty or immediate deployment. He is waiting for us to surrender all to him. He wants to help us with everything, and He is waiting to get out, so let him out as you go! Heal the sick, raise the dead, cast out demons! Freely we have received & freely we give to others!

The Holy Spirit is our intercessor. An intercessor is a person who accesses Heaven and intervenes on behalf of another, especially by prayer.

The Holy Spirit is the Resurrection Power, who raised Jesus from the dead at the command of our Father.

The Holy Spirit is the spirit of God. The Holy Spirit is as much God as Jesus and our Father is. He should be loved, worshiped, honored, and respected, and we should obey the Holy Spirit. We should allow God the Holy Spirit to pray the perfect will of God through us by giving him our tongue. The scripture says to pray without ceasing in 1 Thessalonians 5:17 NKJV. The Holy Spirit, praying through us, helps us carry out this command and builds us up in our most holy faith.

But you, my delightfully loved friends, constantly and progressively build yourselves up on the foundation of your most holy faith by praying every moment in the Spirit. Fasten your hearts to the love of God and receive the mercy of our Lord Jesus Christ, who gives us eternal life.

Jude 1:20-21 TPT

Do you want to move from hindrances to breakthroughs into constant overthrow? Yes! Then let us take dominion in every area of our lives, and everywhere we go. Praying in the spirit is a key to walking in the spirit. Seek the face of Jesus. We are one with the Lord. We have the dominion and power He gave us. Holy Spirit is one with us, and the devils flee! Worship silences the enemy!

The Holy Spirit will never leave us. He is the enforcer of the blessings of our inheritance. We do not have to wait to get to Heaven to partake of our inheritance. The Holy Spirit is the one here for us at all times on the earth. It is a local call to speak with him. Be sure and listen for His voice. Relationships and conversations take two people. A good relationship must have honest communication. So, talk to God about everything. He always listens. He cares deeply about everything you care about. He will answer you. Draw near to God, and He will draw near to you. He is faithful. God tells us to pray so He can answer our prayers.

"Ask, and it will be given to you; seek, and you will find; knock, and it will be opened to you. For everyone who asks receives, and he who seeks finds, and to him who knocks it will be opened. Or what man is there among you who, if his son asks for bread, will give him a stone? Or if he asks for a fish, will he give him a serpent? If you then, being evil, know how to give good gifts to your children, how much more will your Father who is in heaven give good things to those who ask Him!"

Matthew 7:7-11 NKJV

I indeed baptize you with water unto repentance, but He who is coming after me is mightier than I, whose sandals I am not worthy to carry. He will baptize you with the Holy Spirit [a]and fire. His winnowing fan is in His hand, and He will thoroughly clean out His threshing floor, and gather His wheat into the barn, but He will burn up the chaff with unquenchable fire.

Matthew 3:11-12 NKJV

John Baptizes Jesus

Then Jesus came from Galilee to John at the Jordan to be baptized by him. And John tried to prevent Him, saying, "I need to be baptized by You, and are You coming to me?" But Jesus answered

28

and said to him, "Permit it to be so now, for thus it is fitting for us to fulfill all righteousness." Then he allowed Him. When He had been baptized, Jesus came up immediately from the water; and behold, the heavens were opened to Him, and He saw the Spirit of God descending like a dove and alighting upon Him. And suddenly a voice came from heaven, saying, "This is My beloved Son, in whom I am well pleased."

Matthew 13-17 NKJV

Our Heavenly Father only gives good gifts to His children. If you ask Father God to baptize you in the Holy Spirit and fire, He will do it! If Jesus needed to be baptized in water and in the Holy Spirit, how much more do we need this, too? Let God, the Holy Spirit, lead and guide you. Let God, the Holy Spirit, counsel you every day. Let God, the Holy Spirit, heal you of all your past hurts, infirmities, and in every area of your life. Let God, the Holy Spirit, be your best friend. Let God the Holy Spirit love on you and you love on the Holy Spirit. The love of God conquers all! 1 Corinthians 13 says, If I do not have love, it profits me nothing. The love of God conquers all!

I remember who I was with and the exact spot where I stood on the day I received the baptism in the Holy Spirit and Fire. I was at my friend Candy's house in her living room, next to the floor lamp. She told me God will meet you right where you are. I was taken back by this statement. It literally hit me in the heart. I knew it was God speaking to me, and I could not say no to God. At this point, I was crying, and I said, "Yes, I want all that God has for me." Then we prayed a simple, heartfelt prayer, and I literally felt the Holy Spirit come into my belly. It was so supernatural. I will never forget it! Everything was brighter after that moment. The grass and other colors were so vibrant! Literally I went from darkness to light in a moment by the power of the Holy Spirit! God became so real to me, more real than ever before. The Holy Spirit has totally transformed me in every area of my life. I had no idea all the good things God had in store for me and my family —and the best part is, He's not done yet! Praise Jesus!

The baptism in the Holy Spirit is for everyone. To receive the gift of the baptism in the Holy Spirit and fire with the evidence of praying in tongues, please pray this simple prayer, and receive from your Heavenly Father.

Father God in Jesus' name, I invite you to fill me right now to overflowing with your Holy Spirit. I ask you to baptize me with your Holy Spirit and fire with the evidence of speaking in tongues. I want my heavenly language to pray out the perfect will of God today. I thank you for doing it now in Jesus' name.

Now you are filled with the Holy Spirit; He is all over you inside and out. You will feel him rising up on the inside, and then you will need to open your mouth and make a sound. The Holy Spirit is a gentleman. Praying in tongues is a gift that you can start and stop at will. So, open your mouth and start praying in tongues. It may sound silly to you, but it is like a baby when they first start talking. They get a few syllables, followed by some words. When I first started praying in the spirit, it sounded like de de de, da da da, de de de, da da da. This went on for weeks, and then I broke through, starting to get more syllables and words. I have prayed with many people to receive this special baptism, and some people even start by singing in the spirit. This was absolutely beautiful. The more you exercise your new gift of praying in the spirit, the more your language will grow and develop.

I encourage you to pray in the spirit, in the perfect will of God, at all times. Praying in the spirit is talking to God. God is literally talking you up, bragging on you, and praying out your book He wrote about you before you were born. The apostle Paul says I pray in the spirit more than you all. We are going to live longer than Paul, so let us take this challenge to pray more than he did. The Bible tells us that our tongue is like a rudder that steers a ship. Pray in the Spirit to get your freedom and life on track. My God is so good. He will love on you, deliver you, and heal you in every part of yourself that you surrender to him. Doing life God's way has greater rewards. Be willing to lay your will down and do it the Lord's way.

You will see miracles happen in you, then in the lives of those around you.

Pray with me, Holy Spirit, we honor you, have your will, and your way done in us, and through us in Jesus' name. Now, Holy Spirit, what is on your heart? Reveal to us your perfect plan for our lives. We are now available to You. Yield to God and pray in the Spirit now. Let Your kingdom come and Your will be done on earth as it is in Heaven today and every day in Jesus' name, Amen. Praise the Lord! Go in peace and enjoy the release!

3

True Identity

Now, if anyone is enfolded into Christ, he has become an
entirely new person. All that is related to the old order has
vanished.
Behold, everything is fresh and new.
2 Corinthians 5:17 TPT

Who did God create you to be? Are you ready to discover
who you are in Christ? If not now, when? What does understanding
this new revelation mean for your life? God has shown me the
absolute truth that I am an entirely new person, as 2 Corinthians
5:17 says. I believe I am a new person because I have been divinely
transformed from the lost and broken woman I was into the pastor

I am today. Divine transformation is a process that starts when you are born again of the Spirit. The Word of God is true, and in it you can learn your new true identity in Jesus. Your spirit is made new, and now begins the work of saving your soul. Put the old life behind you and run after God, seeking the truth. God will reveal the truth to you. All you have to do is ask Father God to reveal the truth to you now in Jesus' name.

Then God said, "Let us make human beings in our image, to be like us. They will reign over the fish in the sea, the birds in the sky, the livestock, all the wild animals on the earth, and the small animals that scurry along the ground." So God created human beings in his own image. In the image of God he created them; male and female he created them.

Genesis 1:26-27 NLT

We are made in the image and likeness of God, and God gave us authority. Jesus created us male and female. We do not get to choose what gender we are. The scripture says God created us male and female.

Now, may the God of peace and harmony set you apart, making you completely holy. And may your entire being—spirit, soul, and body—be kept completely flawless in the appearing of our Lord

Jesus, the Anointed One. The one who calls you by name is trustworthy and will thoroughly complete his work in you.
1 Thessalonians 5:23-24 TPT

The good work God started in you; He will complete it. He sets you apart. He is the one who makes us holy. God is holy. We are made up of three parts: spirit, soul, and body. As believers, understanding spiritual order is crucial for eradicating sin in our lives and walking in freedom and holiness. We are a spirit, with a soul, housed in a body. When you are born again, your spirit is redeemed. We must work out the salvation of our souls daily. Our soul is made up of three parts: our mind, our will, and our emotions. Our bodies are our earthly suits, and we need them to survive on Earth. We will not need them in Heaven. When we get to Heaven, we will have a new resurrection body. See the scriptures below.

For our citizenship is in heaven, from which we also eagerly wait for the Savior, the Lord Jesus Christ, who will transform our lowly body that it may be conformed to His glorious body, according to the working by which He is able even to subdue all things to Himself.
Philippians 3:20-21 NKJV

The Word of God Discovers Our Condition.

Let us therefore be diligent to enter that rest, lest anyone fall according to the same example of disobedience. For the word of God is living and powerful, and sharper than any two-edged sword, piercing even to the division of soul and spirit, and of joints and marrow, and is a discerner of the thoughts and intents of the heart. And there is no creature hidden from His sight, but all things are naked and open to the eyes of Him to whom we must give account.

Hebrews 4:11-13 NKJV

We must enter into rest and God's peace and stay there. We must pray until we receive the breakthrough of the Lord's peace. God knows everything. It is OK to let Him in and be close to Him. He knows every little detail about you. He cares about every little detail. The word of God will help you and transform you. It will show you where you end, and God begins, and it will bring discipline and correction where you need it. The Word of God is alive, powerful, and sharper than any two-edged sword. The analogy is that it can even separate between joints, bone, and marrow. The Word of God will help you in every area of your life. The Bible is our handbook for life. It is better than any self-help book!

Now, let us look into the book of Ephesians now to unlock your new identity in Christ. The book of Ephesians is a book of love, sacrifice, and prayer. It is our instructions for this life. This book of Ephesians is like our Christian Constitution. I encourage you to meditate on this book of the Bible and allow it to become your reality! The apostle Paul wrote this book to all believers.

Our Sonship and the Father's Plan

Every spiritual blessing in the heavenly realm has already been lavished upon us as a love gift from our wonderful heavenly Father, the Father of our Lord Jesus—all because he sees us wrapped into Christ. This is why we celebrate him with all our hearts! And in love he chose us before he laid the foundation of the universe! Because of his great love, he ordained us so that we would be seen as holy in his eyes with an unstained innocence.

Ephesians 1:3-4 TPT

Here, it states that every spiritual blessing has been lavished upon us. What a wonderful gift from God. This shows us that God is not holding anything back from us, because he sees us through Jesus. We are sons and daughters of the Most High God, the Great God Jehovah. The blood of Jesus completely redeems us. Father God remembers our sins as far as the East is from the West. This means He no longer remembers them. You are forgiven. God chose you to be holy and innocent before the foundation of the universe. This is great love!

For it was always in his perfect plan to adopt us as his delightful children, through our union with Jesus, the Anointed One, so that his tremendous love that cascades over us would glorify his grace —for the same love he has for the Beloved, Jesus, he has for us. And this unfolding plan brings him great pleasure!
Ephesians 1:5-6 TPT

God's perfect plan was to adopt us as His children. He wanted a family, and that's why He created us. Our union with Jesus is the way to the Father. All we have to do is choose Jesus! It is a setup to enjoy eternal life in Heaven with our great Father God. It is by faith through grace that we are saved. It is a gift from God that we cannot earn. We must believe and receive by faith. God loves us with the same love as He has for Jesus.

Since we are now joined to Christ, we have been given the treasures of redemption by his blood—the total cancellation of our sins—all because of the cascading riches of his grace.
Ephesians 1:7 TPT

Our sins are completely gone, canceled, and remembered no more because of His grace. Repent, receive forgiveness, and let anything go that's coming to your mind now. Allow the Holy Spirit to heal you now. You are forgiven. I urge you to forgive yourself. You are forgiven. You are redeemed. This is absolutely true.

This superabundant grace is already powerfully working in us, releasing all forms of wisdom and practical understanding. And through the revelation of the Anointed One, he unveiled his secret desires to us—the hidden mystery of his long-range plan, which he was delighted to implement from the very beginning of time.
Ephesians 1:8-9 TPT

God's superabundant grace is working in us, giving us wisdom and practical understanding. Through the revelation of Jesus, God will share His secret desires with us and His plan, which He purposed from the beginning of time. God wants you to seek Him, and He will share these great treasures of wisdom to you. He wants to be in an intimate relationship with you.

And because of God's unfailing purpose, this detailed plan will reign supreme through every period of time until the fulfillment of all the ages finally reaches its climax—when God makes all things new in all of heaven and earth through Jesus Christ. Through our union with Christ we too have been claimed by God as his own

inheritance. Before we were even born, he gave us our destiny;

that we would fulfill the plan of God who always accomplishes

every purpose and plan in his heart.

Ephesians 1:10-11 TPT

Listen to this: you are God's inheritance. You are God's greatest treasure. The good work that God started in you, He will complete. He has a divine destiny for you. He only needs your yes and your cooperation to complete it. He wants us to be willing and obedient to His plan for our divine destiny. All the plans God has for you are good, giving you hope and a future.

God's purpose was that we Jews, who were the first to long for the

messianic hope, would be the first to believe in the Anointed One

and bring great praise and glory to God! And because of him,

when you who are not Jews heard the revelation of truth, you

believed in the wonderful news of salvation. Now we have been

stamped with the seal of the promised Holy Spirit. He is given to us

like an engagement ring, as the first installment of what's

coming! He is our hope-promise of a future inheritance which seals

us until we have all of redemption's promises and experience

complete freedom—all for the supreme glory and honor of God!

Ephesians 1:12-14 TPT

Salvation was first for the Jews who would believe in Jesus and bring glory to God. Praise God, we see here that those of us who were not Jews and heard the revelation of truth can now receive salvation. We have been grafted in and stamped with the promised seal of the Holy Spirit. It is like a woman who gets an engagement ring. The man has promised to marry her. The Holy Spirit is our engagement ring, and we, the church, are the bride of Christ. He is the proof that Jesus is coming back for us. The Holy Spirit is the promise of our future inheritance. God will do what He says. Glory to God in the highest!

Paul Prays for the Spirit of Wisdom and Revelation
Because of this, since I first heard about your strong faith in the Lord Jesus Christ and your tender love toward all his devoted ones, my heart is always full and overflowing with thanks to God for you as I constantly remember you in my prayers. I pray that the Father of glory, the God of our Lord Jesus Christ, would impart to you the riches of the Spirit of wisdom and the Spirit of revelation to know him through your deepening intimacy with him. I pray that the light of God will illuminate the eyes of your imagination, flooding you with light, until you experience the full revelation of the hope of his calling —that is, the wealth of God's glorious inheritances that he finds in us, his holy ones! I pray that you will continually experience the immeasurable greatness of God's power made

available to you through faith. Then your lives will be an

advertisement of this immense power as it works through you!

This is the mighty power that was released when God raised Christ

from the dead and exalted him to the place of highest honor and

supreme authority in the heavenly realm! And now he is exalted as

first above every ruler, authority, government, and realm of power

in existence! He is gloriously enthroned over every name that is

ever praised, not only in this age but in the age that is coming!

And he alone is the leader and source of everything needed in the

church. God has put everything beneath the authority of Jesus

Christ and has given him the highest rank above all others. And

now we, his church, are his body on the earth and that which fills

him who is being filled by it!

Ephesians 1:15-23 TPT

I encourage you to pray this prayer daily for yourself, your

family, and others in need of salvation. God answers our prayers

when we pray according to the will of God. It brings him great

pleasure and glorifies our Father when we pray according to the will

of God.

But God still loved us with such great love. He is so rich in

compassion and mercy. Even when we were dead and doomed in

our many sins, he united us into the very life of Christ and saved us by his wonderful grace! He raised us up with Christ the exalted

One, and we ascended with him into the glorious perfection and

authority of the heavenly realm, for we are now co-seated as one

with Christ!

Ephesians 2:4-6 TPT

God loves us so much that while we were sinners, He made a way through Jesus Christ to save us with His marvelous grace. This is love; He knew we would mess up, so He prepared a way for us to escape the snare of sin. The Lord provided a way for us to go to Heaven even while we were sinners. God raised us up with Christ, and now we are seated with Christ in the heavenly realms. We are one with God.

Throughout the coming ages we will be the visible display of the

infinite riches of his grace and kindness, which was showered upon

us in Jesus Christ.

Ephesians 2:7 TPT

It says we, you, and me will be the visible display of the infinite riches of his grace that was showered upon us in Jesus Christ. God will put us on display. Wow!

For by grace you have been saved by faith. Nothing you did could ever earn this salvation, for it was the love gift from God that brought us to Christ! So no one will ever be able to boast, for salvation is never a reward for good works or human striving. We have become his poetry, a re-created people that will fulfill the destiny he has given each of us, for we are joined to Jesus, the Anointed One. Even before we were born, God planned in advance our destiny and the good works we would do to fulfill it!
Ephesians 2:8-10 TPT

You are saved by grace through faith. There is no way to earn salvation because it is a gift from God through Christ Jesus. Salvation does not come by good works; it comes by believing in Christ. You will fulfill the destiny God has given to you because you are joined with Jesus the Anointed One. You are His workmanship, created in Christ Jesus for good works. God wrote a book about you before you were born, and you will fulfill your destiny (Psalm 139:16). I pray that you will complete every page written in your book in Heaven in Jesus' name. You are One New Humanity! See the scriptures below.

A New Humanity
So don't forget that you were not born as Jews and were uncircumcised (circumcision itself is just a work of man's hands);

you had none of the Jewish covenants and laws; you were foreigners to Israel's incredible heritage; you were without the covenants and prophetic promises of the Messiah, the promised hope, and without God. Yet look at you now! Everything is new! Although you were once distant and far away from God, now you have been brought delightfully close to him through the sacred blood of Jesus—you have actually been united to Christ! Our reconciling "Peace" is Jesus! He has made Jew and non-Jew one in Christ. By dying as our sacrifice, he has broken down every wall of prejudice that separated us and has now made us equal through our union with Christ. Ethnic hatred has been dissolved by the crucifixion of his precious body on the cross. The legal code that stood condemning every one of us has now been repealed by his command. His triune essence has made peace between us by starting over—forming one new race of humanity, Jews and non-Jews fused together in himself! Two have now become one, and we live restored to God and reconciled in the body of Christ. Through his crucifixion, hatred died. For the Messiah has come to preach this sweet message of peace to you, the ones who were distant, and to those who are near. And now, because we are united to Christ, we both have equal and direct access in the realm of the Holy Spirit to come before the Father! So, you are not foreigners or guests, but rather you are the children of the city of the holy ones, with all the rights as family members of the household of God. You are rising like the perfectly fitted stones of the temple, and your lives have been built up together upon the foundation laid by the apostles and prophets, and best of all, you are connected to the Head Cornerstone of the building, the Anointed One, Jesus Christ himself! This entire building is under construction and is continually growing under his supervision until it rises up completed as the holy temple of the Lord himself. This means that God is transforming each one of you into the Holy of Holies, his dwelling place, through the power of the Holy Spirit living in you!

Ephesians 2:11-22 TPT

We now have equal and direct access, in the spirit through Jesus Christ, to come before our Heavenly Father! This is really Good News. There is no mediator between God and man but Jesus Christ. We are Children of God, adopted into all the rights and privileges as family members of the household of God. The apostles and prophets of the Bible wrote the scriptures. They have laid the foundation for us, and now we build upon it. We are not writing scripture today. We are receiving the word of God within us and gaining revelation from the Holy Spirit. The Holy Spirit is the revealer of the truth. We, the body of Christ, are being built up into the holy temple of the Lord. God is transforming each one of you into the Holy of Holies, His dwelling place, through the power of the

Holy Spirit living in you! We must yield to the Holy Spirit and learn to walk in the Spirit.

Divine Mystery revealed:
Here's the secret: The gospel of grace has made you, non-Jewish
believers, into coheirs of his promise through your union with him.
And you have now become members of his body—one with the
Anointed One!
Ephesians 3:6 TPT

Praise the Lord Jesus Christ for making the only way for everyone to receive salvation through union with Him. We are coheirs with Christ. We have a great inheritance. We are now one with the Lord and members of His body. The gift of the Holy Spirit is our promise of hope.

Now I pray this prayer from the word of God over you:

Paul Prays for Love to Overflow
So I kneel humbly in awe before the Father of our Lord Jesus, the
Messiah, the perfect Father of every father and child in heaven
and on the earth. And I pray that he would unveil within you the
unlimited riches of his glory and favor until supernatural strength
floods your innermost being with his divine might and explosive

power. Then, by constantly using your faith, the life of Christ will be released deep inside you, and the resting place of his love will become the very source and root of your life. Then you will be empowered to discover what every holy one experiences—the great magnitude of the astonishing love of Christ in all its dimensions. How deeply intimate and far-reaching is his love! How enduring and inclusive it is! Endless love beyond measurement that transcends our understanding—this extravagant love pours into you until you are filled to overflowing with the fullness of God! Never doubt God's mighty power to work in you and accomplish all this. He will achieve infinitely more than your greatest request, your most unbelievable dream, and exceed your wildest imagination! He will outdo them all, for his miraculous power constantly energizes you. Now we offer up to God all the glorious praise that rises from every church in every generation through Jesus Christ—and all that will yet be manifest through time and eternity. Amen!

Ephesians 3:14-21 TPT

I encourage you to pray these powerful prayers in Ephesians over yourself and others very often. God is faithful to perform His word in you, your life, and in the lives of those around you. You become what you behold. Behold the Lord Jesus. Sit in His presence now. Allow the Holy Spirit to wrap you up like a warm blanket. God loves you so much. He is willing and able to do exceedingly abundantly above all that you could ever think, ask, or imagine.

Jesus Prays for You

"And I ask not only for these disciples but also for all those who will one day believe in me through their message. I pray for them all to be joined together as one even as you and I, Father, are joined together as one. I pray for them to become one with us so that the world will recognize that you sent me. For the very glory you have given to me I have given them so that they will be joined together as one and experience the same unity that we enjoy. You live fully in me and now I live fully in them so that they will experience perfect unity, and the world will be convinced that you have sent me, for they will see that you love each one of them with the same passionate love that you have for me. "Father, I ask that you allow everyone that you have given to me to be with me where I am! Then they will see my full glory—the very splendor you have placed upon me because you have loved me even before the beginning of time. "You are my righteous Father, but the unbelieving world has never known you in the perfect way that I know you! And all those who believe in me also know that you have sent me! I have revealed to them who you are, and I will continue to make you even more real to them, so that they may

experience the same endless love that you have for me, for your

love will now live in them, even as I live in them!"

John 17:20-26 TPT

Allow yourself to receive the revelation of being one with Father God, one with Jesus Christ, and one with the Holy Spirit. God is alive and real. You can trust the one true living God, Jesus. Take some time, pick up your hands, and sit in His presence now.

The tongue can bring death or life; those who love to talk will reap

the consequences.

Proverbs 18:21 NLT

Pleasant words are like a honeycomb,

Sweetness to the soul and health to the bones.

Proverbs 16:24 NKJV

We see here that the scriptures tell us our words are powerful, capable of bringing death or life. Pleasant words can bring sweetness and healing. I encourage you to change the way you speak about yourself and others. I encourage you to refrain from speaking negatively about anything at all. Speak life over yourself and others. Allow blessings to flow from your tongue. Here are some affirmations to say out loud to yourself regarding who you are now in Christ.

True Identity Affirmations:

I am forgiven.
I am chosen.
I am whole.
I am redeemed.
I am a new creation.
I am more than many sparrows.
I am free from bondage.
I am God's workmanship.
I am an overcomer.
I am a child of God.
I am an heir to the Kingdom of God.
I am fearfully and wonderfully made.
I am a vessel of honor.
I am God's greatest treasure.
I am dead to sin.
I am alive in Christ.
I am a temple of the Holy Spirit.
I am more than a conqueror.
I am healed by Jesus' stripes.
I am fearless and powerful.
I am more than my past.
I am more than what I wear.
I am more than who people say I am.
I am HIS.
I am MADE FOR HIS GLORY!

Give Thanks

Let joy be your continual feast. Make your life a prayer. And in the midst of everything be always giving thanks, for this is God's perfect plan for you in Christ Jesus.

1 Thessalonians 5:16-18 TPT

Don't worry about anything; instead, pray about everything. Tell God what you need and thank him for all he has done. Then you will experience God's peace, which exceeds anything we can understand. His peace will guard your hearts and minds as you live in Christ Jesus.

Philippians 4:6-7 NLT

Thankfulness and gratitude are a believer's mindset and way of life. It is literally God's will for your life. I encourage you to wake up, be grateful, and thank the Lord that He woke you up today. No day on this Earth is promised. Every day is a gift from God. When you are grateful, there is no room for complaining. They are polar opposites. Practice being truly grateful and thankful. Here is a list of things to get you started.

Thank you for the air I breathe.

Thank you for leading me every step of the way.

Thank you for forgiving me.

Thank you for always listening to me.

Thank you for adopting me into your family.

Thank you that I am a child of God. I am loved, valued, and safe.

Thank you for always being so good to me.

Thank you for your Mercy and Grace.

Thank you for restoring me and my family.

Thank you, Lord, for everything.

Now, tell God anything else you want to give Him thanks for.

4

Supernatural Acceleration

"But when the truth-giving Spirit comes, he will unveil the reality of every truth within you. He will not speak on his own, but only what he hears from the Father, and he will reveal prophetically to you what is to come. He will glorify me on the earth, for he will receive from me what is mine and reveal it to you. Everything that belongs to the Father belongs to me—that's why I say that the Divine Encourager will receive what is mine and reveal it to you."

John 16:13-15 TPT

Are you ready for God to catch you up? Are you ready for more truth? If not now, when? Buckle up and get ready for more supernatural revelation from the Holy Spirit! He will unveil the reality of every truth within you. The Holy Spirit only speaks what He hears from the Father. So, when you're hearing from the Holy Spirit, you're hearing from your heavenly Father! You have a Direct Line to your Father God! The Holy Spirit is only going to glorify God. The Divine Encourager will receive what is Jesus' and reveal it to you. This tells us that God is not hiding things from us; He wants to reveal them to us through the Holy Spirit.

Our God is supernatural. There is nothing just natural about Him. He is the Creator of the universe! He creates something out of nothing. He speaks and creates anything He wants. God is not bound by the laws of this natural realm we live in.

Acceleration is the increase in something's speed, or its ability to go faster; the increase in the speed at which something happens; the rate at which something moves more quickly or happens faster or sooner.

Supernatural Acceleration is God redeeming the time in your life by propelling you into your future as you immerse yourself in seeking Him, learning about Him, and His Kingdom. If you draw near to God, He will draw near to you. If you delight yourself in the Lord, He will give you the desires of your heart (Ps. 37:4). The Kingdom of God is always advancing. So, we should be advancing too. We should be learning about God and our purpose, and working to fulfill our destiny. It doesn't matter how old you are when you receive the Lord. As you surrender, God will supernaturally accelerate your process and catch you up right where He needs you to be. All of our mistakes have been factored in. So, if you immerse yourself in the Lord, you will supernaturally accelerate your process. I like to call it Jesus boot camp. Drop what you are doing and go after God! Turn off the secular television and radio, and any other activities that you may be filling your time with, and go after God. It will be the best thing you ever did for yourself, your family, your business or job, your relationships, your finances, and your ministry. Drop what you're doing and GO AFTER GOD!

Carve a special time out to sit alone with God. During this time, you can pray in English, lifting up the Lord. Thank Him. Talk to Him about everything. Share your innermost thoughts and desires with Him. Sing to Him. Tell Him what He said in the Word of God. As you create this atmosphere of being still and quiet, be sure to listen to what the Lord is saying to you. God mostly speaks in a still, quiet voice. This is how He leads and guides us. Communication is essential in any relationship, especially with God. Pray in tongues, often. Reading and meditating on the Word of God is especially important. This is how we get to know God. We learn what He likes and what He hates. Reading the Word of God and receiving revelation from the Holy Spirit renews and transforms our minds. Making your appointments with God will help you have fewer disappointments in this life.

"And everything I've taught you is so that the peace which is in me will be in you and will give you great confidence as you rest in me. For in this unbelieving world, you will experience trouble and sorrows, but you must be courageous, for I have conquered the world!"

John 16:33 TPT

Jesus is the Prince of Peace, and He gives us His supernatural peace as we rest in Him. He teaches us how to live, move, and have our being in Him. This will bring you great joy and peace. Even though in this world we will have trouble and sorrow, we must always remember to be courageous, for Jesus has already conquered the world. We will overcome evil because Jesus overcame it.

"And when you pray, you shall not be like the hypocrites. For they love to pray standing in the synagogues and on the corners of the streets, that they may be seen by men. Assuredly, I say to you, they have their reward. But you, when you pray, go into your room, and when you have shut your door, pray to your Father who is in the secret place; and your Father who sees in secret will reward you openly. And when you pray, do not use vain

repetitions as the heathen do. For they think that they will be heard for their many words. "Therefore do not be like them. For your Father knows the things you have need of before you ask Him. In this manner, therefore, pray: Our Father in heaven, Hallowed be Your name. Your kingdom come. Your will be done on earth as it is in heaven. Give us this day our daily bread. And forgive us our debts, As we forgive our debtors. And do not lead us into temptation, but deliver us from the evil one. For Yours is the kingdom and the power and the glory forever. Amen. "For if you forgive men their trespasses, your heavenly Father will also forgive you. But if you do not forgive men their trespasses, neither will your Father forgive your trespasses."

Matthew 6:5-15 NKJV

This passage of scripture contains many keys.

1. It says when you pray, not if you pray.
2. Go and be alone with God...no distractions.
3. Pray to him in the secret place.
4. Your Father who sees you in secret will reward you openly.
5. Don't speak empty words but pray from your heart meaning what you say.

6. Jesus told us to pray like this, and He gave us the Our Father Prayer. It is not to be prayed as a repetitious prayer, but from the heart. It can also serve as a model for praying as Jesus did.

   a. I lift Father God up and bless His holy name.

   b. Tell the Lord, your Kingdom come manifest here and now; Your will be done right here and now on this Earth as it is in Heaven.

   c. You are my provider, Lord, you are all I need; you are all I want.

   d. I release forgiveness to anyone known or unknown who's ever hurt, offended, or caused me or my family pain, and forgive me, Father for wrong actions, deeds, words, and thoughts.

   e. Rescue me from tribulations and deliver me Lord from every evil.

   f. For yours is the Kingdom, the power, and the glory now and forever in Jesus' name. Amen.

7. When you pray, you must release forgiveness to others so that your Heavenly Father will forgive you for your wrongs.

8. The scripture clearly states that if you do not forgive others, God will not forgive you. This is huge and I think many people overlook this and hold on to unforgiveness.

I believe it's in our best interest to forgive. It will release you from the power of unforgiveness and offense. Forgiving will keep you in the love, peace, and presence of God.

When you pray in this way, you will begin to notice a shift and change within yourself. The Holy Spirit will help you forgive people, so lean on Him when you need Him. He's your comforter, advocate, and helper. He's your best friend, always there to answer the phone when you call! He's always there at any moment ready to help you. He's always ready for you to yield to Him to pray the perfect prayers.

"So above all, constantly seek God's kingdom and His righteousness, then all these less important things will be given to you abundantly. Refuse to worry about tomorrow, but deal with each challenge that comes your way, one day at a time.

Tomorrow will take care of itself."

Matthew 6:33-34 TPT

This scripture is one of my favorites. God has shown Himself faithful time and time again. If you seek first the Kingdom of God and His righteousness, everything shall be added to you, to your house, to your family, and to your ministry. We must not worry about the future. Remember that God has everything worked out for good to those who love God and are called according to His purpose. This reminds me of a testimony of the goodness of God. I started working on my associate degree through Warrior Notes School of Ministry. I didn't tell anyone I started doing this at first, because I was a quitter for most of my life. I would start college only to have a train wreck happen in my life, and then I would quit. I had less than $1500 a month coming in. I started tithing and paying for the college courses. There was absolutely no way I could afford either one, but God supernaturally made it work. I couldn't afford to tithe until I started tithing. By the grace of God, every month I had enough money to pay my bills, buy groceries, tithe, and pay for my college courses! This supernaturally went on until I received my bachelor's degree! Miracles upon miracles! Praise Jesus! So, whatever you need in any area, if you seek first the Kingdom of God and His righteousness everything shall be added to you! My Father God is so good and faithful. What He did for me, I pray He does for you even more exceedingly abundantly above all that you could ask, think, or imagine! In Jesus' name, amen!

There is no greater love than to lay down one's life for one's friends. You are my friends if you do what I command. I no longer call you slaves, because a master doesn't confide in his slaves. Now you are my friends, since I have told you everything the Father told me. You did not choose me. I chose you. I appointed you to go and produce lasting fruit so that the Father will give you whatever you ask for, using my name. This is my command: Love each other.

John 15:13-17 NLT

The whole chapter of John 15 is all about the fruit of prayer. Here, Jesus calls us His friends because He laid down His life for us. Jesus said, "You are my friends if you do what I command." Jesus will tell us everything the Father has told Him. Jesus chose and appointed us to produce lasting fruit through prayer. Jesus tells us how to pray: we ask our Father in Jesus' name, and we shall have what we ask for. So, it's straightforward: we believe and pray to our Heavenly Father in the name of His Son, Jesus, and we receive what we ask for. Then He commands us to love each other.

Pray in the Spirit at all times and on every occasion. Stay alert and be persistent in your prayers for all believers everywhere.

Ephesians 6:18 NLT

You can literally make your life a prayer. Do everything unto the Lord. When praying in the spirit, you are praying the perfect will of God for your life and the lives of others. God will build you up and strengthen you. Praying in the spirit totally bypasses your mind, where we speak from. There have been studies that were conducted by doctors that proved praying in tongues activates a different part of the brain. So, you can pray in the spirit while working or reading. You can multitask while praying in the spirit! This is so supernatural. Build yourself up in your most holy faith by praying in the Spirit and keeping yourself safe in the love of God. (Jude 1:20-21) The more you pray in the spirit, the easier it becomes to do other things simultaneously.

And in a similar way, the Holy Spirit takes hold of us in our human frailty to empower us in our weakness. For example, at times we don't even know how to pray or know the best things to ask for. But the Holy Spirit rises up within us to super-intercede on our behalf, pleading to God with emotional sighs too deep for words. God, the searcher of the heart, knows fully our longings, yet he also understands the desires of the Spirit, because the Holy Spirit passionately pleads before God for us, his holy ones, in perfect harmony with God's plan and our destiny. So we are convinced that every detail of our lives is continually woven together for good, for we are his lovers who have been called to fulfill his designed purpose.

Romans 8:26-28 TPT

Here we see that if we don't know what to pray, we yield to the Holy Spirit, and He rises up and super-intercedes on our behalf pleading to God. And God knows everything about us. He also knows the desires of His Spirit because the Holy Spirit passionately pleads for us before God in perfect harmony with God's plan and our destiny. God will work out every detail for good to those who love God and have been called to fulfill His divine purpose. Remember, God wrote a book about you before you were born (Psalms 139:16). I encourage you to pray in the spirit all the time, as much as you can. Put the word of God before you too. You can put reminders in your phone or make sticky notes or index cards with the word of God on them to review the scriptures. The word of God will come alive to you. This will accelerate your process with the Lord.

But continue to grow and increase in God's grace and intimacy with our Lord and Savior, Jesus Christ. May he receive all the glory both now and until the day eternity begins. Amen!

2 Peter 3:18 TPT

As you mature and grow spiritually, you will yield to the grace of God and develop a genuine passion to know Jesus Christ intimately. Over time, we transform into His beautiful image. You become what you behold. You didn't become who you are overnight, so it's understandable that it takes time to grow and change. The good news is that the time it takes depends entirely on your willingness to yield and surrender. The more you surrender to and immerse yourself in the Lord, the more your sanctification process will be supernaturally accelerated.

Put on your new nature, and be renewed as you learn
to know your Creator and become like him.
Colossians 3:10 NLT

The more we seek and become closer to God, the more we become like Him. Your desires will change from wanting sinful, fleshly things and ways to enjoying good, godly ways as you renew your mind with the word of God. You will want to do things God's way as you get closer to Him. Building a relationship takes time. We must make time for God; He will not push Himself on us. He will not force us to do anything. We choose to make time for him daily. I encourage you to say yes to God every day.

The Power of Your Words

We all fail in many areas, but especially with our words. Yet if we're able to bridle the words we say we are powerful enough to control ourselves in every way, and that means our character is mature and fully developed. Horses have bits and bridles in their mouths so that we can control and guide their large body. And the same with mighty ships, though they are massive and driven by fierce winds, yet they are steered by a tiny rudder at the direction of the person at the helm. And so the tongue is a small part of the body, yet it carries great power! Just think of how a small flame can set a huge forest ablaze. And the tongue is a fire! It can be compared to the sum total of wickedness and is the most dangerous part of our human body. It corrupts the entire body and is a hellish flame! It releases a fire that can burn throughout the course of human existence. For every wild animal on earth including birds, creeping reptiles, and creatures of the sea and land have all been overpowered and tamed by humans, but the tongue is not able to be tamed. It is a fickle, unrestrained evil that spews out words full of toxic poison! We use our tongue to praise God our Father and then turn around and curse a person who was made in his very image! Out of the same mouth we pour out words of praise one minute and curses the next. My brothers and sisters, this should never be!   James 3:2-10 TPT

We see here in this passage that our words matter. Our tongue is like the rudder of a ship. The small rudder of a ship controls where it goes, just like our tongues control where we go. We must use our tongues to speak where God is telling us to go. Speak blessings, not curses, over yourself and others. We are all made in the Image of God, and we should not be cursing anyone made in God's image. The Lord wills for everyone to go to Heaven. Do not hinder yourself or anyone in their process by cursing or speaking negatively about them. You have control of what comes out of your mouth. Slow down and be slow to speak. Speak life over every area of your life and the lives of others. You reap what you sow. Sow blessings!

"A good man out of the good treasure of his heart brings forth good things, and an evil man out of the evil treasure brings forth evil things. But I say to you that for every idle word men may speak, they will give account of it in the day of judgment. For by your words, you will be justified, and by your words you will be condemned."

Matthew 12:35-37 NKJV

According to these scriptures, we receive the revelation that we will be held accountable on the day of judgment for every idle word we speak. We must get our tongues under control. We repent for speaking idle words, Lord. Help us every day to speak Your will and where we are going. Praying in the Spirit and meditating on the word of God will help you do this. You have control of what you say. If it is not something good, hold off on speaking. Begin making decisions in your life that align with the Word of God. Isaiah 55:11 says, "So shall My word be that goes forth from My mouth; It shall not return to Me void, but it shall accomplish what I please, and it shall prosper in the thing for which I sent it." God will perform His word, so believe it and declare it. Then watch it come to pass! Hallelujah!

In the beginning, God created the heavens and the earth. The earth was formless and empty, and darkness covered the deep waters. And the Spirit of God was hovering over the surface of the waters. Then God said, "Let there be light," and there was light. And God saw that the light was good. Then he separated the light from the darkness. God called the light "day" and the darkness "night." And evening passed and morning came, marking the first day.

Genesis 1:1-5 NLT

God speaks and He creates. This is how He created us to be as well. We are made in His image, and we are supposed to do as our Father does. Just like children want to do what their parents do, we should do only what our Heavenly Father is doing. Be encouraged, we are creators too, just like our Heavenly Father! Speak where you are going. Don't dwell on the past or where you are right now. Speak life and blessings. Declare what the Word of God says over your situation.

Fasting

"When you fast, do not look gloomy and pretend to be spiritual. They want everyone to know they're fasting, so they appear in public looking miserable and disheveled. Believe me, they've already received their reward. When you fast, don't let it be obvious, but instead, wash your face and groom yourself and realize that your Father in the secret place is the one who is watching all that you do in secret and will continue to reward you."

Matthew 6:16-18 TPT

We must incorporate fasting into our lifestyle. Here we see that the Word says, "When you fast, not if you fast." So, when you fast, do not announce it to the world, proclaim it to God and your Father who sees what you do in secret will reward you openly. Fasting and prayer will draw you closer to God. It will empty you of yourself, and God will be able to come in and deliver and heal you of many things from your past like rejection, unforgiveness, shame, trauma, fear, addictions of all kinds, guilt, grief, and anything else you may be dealing with. There are some things He will do for you without you even realizing it. If God reveals something that happened in your past, turn it over to Him because He wants to heal you in that area. Do not be fearful, yield to the Holy Spirit, and allow Him to work in you even right now. Stop and yield to Him and receive your freedom in Jesus' name. Anything that the Lord heals you of personally is the very thing you will be able to help others break free from, and more! You see Father God wants to help you, and then He will want you to turn around and help others! It is a beautiful chain reaction. You will make history by obeying God in your walk and then helping others do the same!

Then Jesus said to his disciples, "If you truly want to follow me, you should at once completely reject and disown your own life. And you must be willing to share my cross and experience it as your own, as you continually surrender to my ways. For if you choose self-sacrifice and lose your lives for my glory, you will continually discover true life. But if you choose to keep your lives

for yourselves, you will forfeit what you try to keep."

Matthew 16:24-25 TPT

Here we see that God is telling us that we must surrender our will and choose His will to discover true life. You may think this is a hard thing, but God is concerned about your heart. He wants all of you not just a part of you. Everything you sacrifice does not go unnoticed by God. The plans and purpose He has for your life are way better than anything you may think at this very moment. God will work in you and through you all for His good pleasure. All for the glory of God. He will make you look really good for His glory!

Paul's Disciplined Lifestyle

Isn't it obvious that all runners on the racetrack keep on running to win, but only one receives the victor's prize? Yet each one of you must run the race to be victorious. A true athlete will be disciplined in every respect, practicing constant self-control in order to win a laurel wreath that quickly withers. But we run our race to win a victor's crown that will last forever. For that reason, I don't run just for exercise or box like one throwing aimless punches, but I train like a champion athlete. I subdue my body and get it under my control so that after preaching the good news to others I myself won't be disqualified.

1 Corinthians 9:24-27 TPT

Here, Paul is speaking about a disciplined lifestyle. We must undergo change and transformation, and this requires discipline. Just as a champion athlete must be highly focused and disciplined to win a race, so too must one be in order to succeed. We must subdue our bodies and get them under control, so we are not disqualified. The grace of God will help you to be successful in this area if you surrender your will to His. Your spirit will grow and be in charge of your soul and your body with the leadership of the Holy Spirit. You may not understand it all right now, but as you yield to God and do what the scriptures say, your understanding will be enlightened, and you will be divinely transformed. You will move from glory to glory by the revelations from the spirit of the living God.

Now we will go over a passage of scripture in the book of Galatians. The book of Galatians really helped me to get my mind right. I believe it will help you transform, too.

The Holy Spirit, Our Victory

Let me emphasize this: As you yield to the dynamic life and power of the Holy Spirit, you will abandon the cravings of your self-life. When your self-life craves the things that offend the Holy Spirit, you hinder him from living free within you! And the Holy Spirit's intense cravings hinder your self-life from dominating you! So then, the two incompatible and conflicting forces within you are your self-life of the flesh and the new creation life of the Spirit.

Galatians 5:16-17 TPT

We must yield to the life and the power of the Holy Spirit and abandon the cravings of your self-life. We don't want to offend the Holy Spirit by living in the flesh. We want God to live in us freely and fully. So, the Holy Spirit's intense cravings will hinder your self-life from overtaking you. The flesh and the new creation spirit life are incompatible. The flesh must submit to the spirit of God as you yield to Him. Surrendering is the key. Right now lay down your pride, admit that God knows more than you and you want to do things His way from now on.

But when you yield to the life of the Spirit, you will no longer be living under the law, but soaring above it!

Galatians 5:18 TPT

73

When you yield to the life of the Spirit, you will no longer be bound, but you will be walking in love and yielding to God and soaring above the law. Jesus came to fulfill the law. You won't be fulfilling the lust of the flesh and working against God as you yield and become free by the spirit of the living God. Remember, change and divine transformation take time. Be loving and give yourself some grace to grow. God is with you, and He will never leave you. He will be there to guide you every step of the way. He is so good! God's grace is sufficient for you.

The behavior of the self-life is obvious: Sexual immorality, lustful thoughts, pornography, chasing after things instead of God, manipulating others, hatred of those who get in your way, senseless arguments, resentment when others are favored, temper tantrums, angry quarrels, only thinking of yourself, being in love with your own opinions, being envious of the blessings of others, murder, uncontrolled addictions, wild parties, and all other similar behavior. Haven't I already warned you that those who use their "freedom" for these things will not inherit the kingdom realm of God!

Galatians 5:19-21 TPT

In this passage of scripture, we see that the behavior of the self-life is clearly stated, and God says that people who use their freedom for any of these things will not inherit the Kingdom of God. They are sexual immorality, lustful thoughts, pornography, chasing after things instead of God, manipulating others, hatred of those who get in your way, senseless arguments, resentment when others are favored, temper tantrums, angry quarrels, only thinking of yourself, being in love with your own opinions, being envious of the blessings of others, murder, uncontrolled addictions, wild parties, and all other similar behaviors. So, God said if we do any of these things or anything like them, we will not inherit the Kingdom of God. Remember, if you are doing any of these things now, surrender them to God and make up your mind not to do them anymore; God will help you. He is full of mercy and grace. It is God's pleasure to help you overcome all these and more. The more you seek after God, the less you will want to do any of these dirty things. Allow God to come in with His holy fire and cleanse you of all these and all unrighteousness. Ask Him now, Father God, in Jesus' name, fill me, cleanse me with Your holy fire of all unrighteousness and uncleanliness. Deliver me and heal me right now by the power of Your Holy Spirit. Thank you, Lord, for working in me, in Jesus' name, Amen.

But the fruit produced by the Holy Spirit within you is divine love in all its varied expressions: joy that overflows, peace that subdues, patience that endures, kindness in action, a life full of virtue, faith that prevails, gentleness of heart, and strength of spirit. Never set the law above these qualities, for they are meant to be limitless.

Galatians 5:22-23 TPT

Now we see the fruit of the spirit working within you is divine love, joy, peace, patience, kindness, a life full of virtue, faith, gentleness of heart, goodness, and strength of spirit, which is also self-control. These qualities are meant to be limitless. These are the qualities of God, and we should have all these same qualities. The more you yield to God, the more your character will grow, and these qualities will be more prevalent in you. You become what you behold.

Keep in mind that we who belong to Jesus Christ have already experienced crucifixion. For everything connected with our self-life was put to death on the cross and crucified with Messiah. If the Spirit is the source of our life, we must also allow the Spirit to direct every aspect of our lives. So may we never be arrogant, or look down on another, for each of us is an original. We must

forsake all jealousy that diminishes the value of others.

Galatians 5:24-26 TPT

I hope you are beginning to see that you belong to Jesus Christ, and He desires to live His life in and through you, all for His glory. The Holy Spirit is our source of life, and we must allow Him to direct every area of our lives. We need to follow the leading of the Holy Spirit. We must not be jealous of others or look down on them, for we are all made in the image of God, and God wants everyone to come to the saving knowledge of Jesus Christ. Jesus is the answer to all of our problems. If you see someone lacking in an area, most likely they need Jesus. We all need Jesus. So, pray for their salvation, pray for God to reveal Himself to them, and make them whole in their spirit, soul, and body.

Meditating on the word of God is so important. Through this process, as you pray and fast, you should also meditate on the word of God. This combination is a key to walking in the spirit. As you read this book, you are meditating on the Word of God and receiving revelation upon revelation by the Holy Spirit.

The Son Gives Freedom

Jesus said to those Jews who believed in him, "When you continue to embrace all that I teach, you prove that you are my true followers. 32 For if you embrace the: truth, it will release true freedom into your lives."

John 8:31-32 TPT

The Truth Shall Make You Free

Then Jesus said to those Jews who believed Him, "If you abide in My word, you are My disciples indeed. And you shall know the truth, and the truth shall make you free."

John 8:31-32 NKJV

Here I have put two versions of the same scripture. This will help you gain a deeper understanding of what God is saying. As you meditate on the scriptures, compare different versions of the Bible, and the scriptures will start to come alive to you. You will be able to grasp what the Lord is saying. I like to use The Passion Translation, The New King James Version, The Amplified Classic, and The New Living Translation. Sometimes I use the English Standard Version and the Geneva Bible too.

When you embrace all that Jesus teaches and abide in the word of God, you show Him that you are His true disciples. Embracing the truth of God's word will bring freedom into your life. Knowing the truth shall make you free. Whom the Son sets free is free indeed! Hallelujah!

I will list several additional passages of scripture that I believe will help you supernaturally accelerate your process at the end of this chapter. You want to get your wisdom and understanding from the whole counsel of God. The Bible says the fear of the Lord is the beginning of wisdom. This is not an earthly fear of being scared. This is a reverence for knowing that God is God and you are not, respecting, submitting to, and obeying the one true living God. Do you want to know the entire truth? Ask him to reveal it to you now in Jesus' name. Please pray in the spirit, read, and meditate on the word of God, and incorporate fasting into your lifestyle. I also want to encourage you to deepen your learning about the Lord by enrolling in the Warrior Notes School of Ministry. Full immersion is the key. It will significantly help you receive revelations and impartations from the Lord. By doing all of these things and making your daily appointments with the Lord, you will change and transform into the person God created you to be. As you journey to discover God, seek out on fire for God people who can help you grow. The Lord will help you find your God family or your tribe!

How God anointed Jesus of Nazareth with the Holy Spirit and with power, who went about doing good and healing all who were oppressed by the devil, for God was with Him.

Acts 10:38 NKJV

God will supernaturally put people in your path that He wants to bless and help. Jesus showed us how to walk in the Spirit, doing good and healing all whom the devil oppresses, because God was with Him. Now, God is with you, empowering you to walk like Jesus did. He will supernaturally empower and propel you to walk out your divine destiny, as written in your book in Heaven. I like to call it God Adventures. It is the most fun I have ever had in life doing exploits for God! God wants everyone to receive healing and wholeness because it is the victory He accomplished on the cross.

As you grow in the Lord, you must move from having head knowledge to experiential knowledge of God's word. Believing the Word must move from your head to your heart. This is why meditating on the word of God and allowing the Holy Spirit to reveal the scriptures to you is so important. It's a transaction that occurs in your spirit, then extends to your soul and body. Your soul and body must align with the word of God. Here are a few scriptures to meditate on for healing.

Surely He has borne our griefs And carried our sorrows; Yet we esteemed Him stricken, Smitten by God, and afflicted. 5 But He was wounded for our transgressions, He was bruised for our iniquities; The chastisement for our peace was upon Him, and by His stripes we are healed.

Isaiah 53:4-5 NKJV

When evening had come, they brought to Him many who were demon-possessed. And He cast out the spirits with a word, and healed all who were sick, that it might be fulfilled which was spoken by Isaiah the prophet, saying: "He Himself took our infirmities And bore our sicknesses."

Matthew 8:16-17 NKJV

who Himself bore our sins in His own body on the tree, that we, having died to sins, might live for righteousness—by whose stripes you were healed.

1 Peter 2:24 NKJV

He sent out his word and healed them, snatching them from the door of death.

Psalms 107:20 NLT

Since you have heard about Jesus and have learned the truth that comes from him, throw off your old sinful nature and your former way of life, which is corrupted by lust and deception. Instead, let the Spirit renew your thoughts and attitudes. Put on your new nature, created to be like God—truly righteous and holy.
Ephesians 4:21-24 NLT

Here are more passages of scripture listed below to look up and meditate on. By doing what the word of God says to do, put off your old sinful nature and renew your mind with the word of God, you will put on your new nature and be changed and transformed in the way you think. Your whole life will change for the better. Your perspective will become higher and more godly. Remember to look up the scriptures in the different versions to gain a deeper understanding and wisdom of the Word of God. Take it slow, read word for word—one or two verses at a time. Look up the meaning of the words that stand out to you or the ones you do not know the meaning of. Look up the root meaning of the words. There are many treasures to find in the Word of God. It is the glory of God to hide; it is the glory of kings to seek and find (Proverbs 25:2). God wants us to dig into the Word of God for more revelation. Write down the revelations the Lord gives you. They are great treasures! Regularly review the revelations as you renew your mind with the word of

God. Divine Transformation is yours! Keep going after God! Now is the time!

1 John 4

Ephesians 1-6

John 1, 14-17

Psalms 23, 91, 119, 139

Romans 5, 6, 8, 12

Matthew 5-6

Nemiah 8:10

Proverbs 1, 2, 3, 6

1 Corinthians 12-14

2 Corinthians 5

Galatians 5

James 1-5

Jude 1

Philippians 3-4

Hebrews 12

2 Thessalonians 2

2 Timothy 1-4

5

Overcome Your Past

Behold, I stand at the door and knock. If anyone hears My voice and opens the door, I will come in to him and dine with him, and he with Me. To him who overcomes I will grant to sit with Me on My throne, as I also overcame and sat down with My Father on His throne.

Revelation 3:20-21 TPT

When will it ever be the right time? If not now, when? What's been holding you back? Is it bitterness, unforgiveness, and anger? Forgiveness is a huge part of overcoming your past and moving forward with the Lord. Remember, God is so good. Open yourself up to the Lord. He is waiting for you to invite Him into every area of your life and within yourself. The Holy Spirit is a gentleman. God gave us free will, so we must ask Him in. Ask the Holy Spirit for help. Help is the shortest prayer I pray, and I pray it every day. I can do nothing without the Lord, nor do I want to. He is always there, ready and available to help you and me. He came and conquered the enemy and made a way for us to overcome. Now He is telling us that He will reward us for doing our part and overcoming! The reward is to sit with Jesus on His throne!

I hope you have received the revelation that you are a child of God, and greater is God in you than the devil who is in the world (1 John 4:4). You are God's Greatest Treasure. He wants you free. He wants you whole. He wants to heal you of all of your past traumas. When you repented and were born again, the Lord forgave you of all your past sins. He forgave you for every little thing. You must release yourself from your past by forgiving yourself. Surrender yourself to the Lord. Whatever the Holy Spirit reveals, He will heal.

Definition of forgiven from Merriam-Webster's dictionary: to cease to have feelings of anger or bitterness toward someone.

He does not punish us for all our sins; He does not deal harshly with us, as we deserve. For his unfailing love toward those who fear him is as great as the height of the heavens above the earth. He has removed our sins as far from us as the east is from the west. The Lord is like a father to his children, tender and compassionate to those who fear him.

Psalms 103:10-13 NLT

Our God is compassionate and merciful. He has no record of our past sins. The blood of Jesus has wiped them away. The blood of Jesus cleanses us from all unrighteousness. Father God has removed our sins as far as the East is from the West. Picture a globe of the Earth. If you go North, eventually you will end up traveling South. If you go East, you will always be going East. If you travel West, you would always be going West. East and West never turn into each other. So, from this analogy, we see that God removed our sins and remembers them no more. So, repent, receive and release forgiveness to yourself now in Jesus' name. Let yourself be unhooked from sins snare. You are forgiven. You are redeemed. Christ paid it all for you.

So now there is no condemnation for those who belong to Christ Jesus. And because you belong to him, the power of the life-giving Spirit has freed you from the power of sin that leads to death.

Romans 8:1-2 NLT

You must get this: there is no condemnation against you, and the case is closed. You belong to Jesus, you are free, you are forgiven, and you are redeemed. The power of the Holy Spirit has freed you from the power of sin that leads to death. Romans 8 is the template for your spiritual life. Meditate often on the whole chapter of Romans 8 and allow God to reveal it to you.

Children, obey your parents in the Lord [that is, accept their guidance and discipline as His representatives], for this is right [for obedience teaches wisdom and self-discipline]. Honor [esteem, value as precious] your father and your mother [and be respectful to them]—this is the first commandment with a promise— so that it may be well with you, and that you may have a long life on the earth.

Ephesians 6:1-3 AMP

Obedience brings about the Lord's blessings in our lives. It is essential to honor your parents and take care of them. Here, we see it's straightforward in the scripture. There's a commandment with a promise that if you obey God and honor your parents, it will be well with you and you will live long on the Earth. In this life, we reap what we sow, so sow into your future. Follow the path God has set for you. Submit to the Lord and walk in His supernatural power. When you are under authority, you will walk in great authority.

The Whole Armor of God

A final word: Be strong in the Lord and in his mighty power. Put on all of God's armor so that you will be able to stand firm against all strategies of the devil. For we are not fighting against flesh-and-blood enemies, but against evil rulers and authorities of the unseen world, against mighty powers in this dark world, and against evil spirits in the heavenly places. Therefore, put on every piece of God's armor so you will be able to resist the enemy in the time of evil. Then, after the battle, you will still be standing firm. Stand your ground, putting on the belt of truth and the body armor of God's righteousness. For shoes, put on the peace that comes from the Good News so that you will be fully prepared. In addition to all of these, hold up the shield of faith to stop the fiery arrows of the devil. Put on salvation as your helmet, and take the sword of the Spirit, which is the word of God. Pray in the Spirit at all times and on every occasion. Stay alert and be persistent in your prayers for all believers everywhere.

Ephesians 6:10-18 NLT

I encourage you to meditate on this whole passage. Get these truths inside of you and manifest the armor of God in the way you live. Armor is not just something you put on; it is who you are. The Word of God will manifest in you and through you as you meditate and receive revelations of it. In verse 12, it says that we are not fighting against flesh-and-blood enemies, but against evil rulers and authorities of the unseen world, against mighty powers in this dark world, and evil spirits in the heavenly places. This passage of scripture was life-changing for me. I pray it is for you, too. We are NOT fighting against people. You are NOT fighting against your brother or sister in Christ. The devil uses people like puppets to attack us. So, you may think Sally said this about me or David did this to me, but really, it was the devil behind the whole thing. Once I received this revelation, it became easier to forgive people right away because I now know the devil is using them. Most people had no idea they were doing the devil's work. I did not think I was on the wrong team until I chose team Jesus! Knowing this revelation made it easier to love and forgive people through hard times and circumstances. The love of God casts out fear. The love of God will disarm the enemy that is working through people so that you can minister life to them.

You must also forgive others for any wrongs that were committed against you. Releasing forgiveness to others makes you free. Harboring unforgiveness can make you sick in your body and your mind. For example, I used to have terrible arthritis in my hands. I would take so many Midol to help with this pain, swelling, and inflammation. I had fat sausage fingers that hurt whether I would bend them or not. God revealed to me that this was from unforgiveness towards my ex-husband. I released him to the Lord and forgave him, and immediately, arthritis left my hands, and it never returned! Praise God, thank you, Lord, you are my healer! Thank you! You are my everything! What is the Lord revealing to you now? Who do you need to forgive? Release them to the Lord now and receive the healing you need in your body in Jesus' name! What Jesus did for me, He will do for you, too!

Here are some scriptures on forgiveness for you to meditate on:

Love prospers when a fault is forgiven, but dwelling on it separates close friends.

Proverbs 17:9 NLT

Love others well by forgiving them of their faults. Love covers many sins. See the good in others because dwelling on the bad separates close friends. No one is perfect. We all need God's grace and mercy to grow and mature.

And do not bring sorrow to God's Holy Spirit by the way you live. Remember, he has identified you as his own, guaranteeing that you will be saved on the day of redemption. Get rid of all bitterness, rage, anger, harsh words, and slander, as well as all types of evil behavior. Instead, be kind to each other, tenderhearted, forgiving one another, just as God through Christ has forgiven you.

Ephesians 4:30-32 NLT

Let us bring great joy by the way that we live to the Holy Spirit. Remember, He is our promise that Jesus is coming again. Put away all these evil behaviors and be kind, generous, and tender-hearted, forgiving your brother or your sister just as God has forgiven you.

Then Peter came to him and asked, "Lord, how often should I forgive someone who sins against me? Seven times?" "No, not seven times," Jesus replied, "but seventy times seven!

Matthew 18:21-22 NLT

Jesus says we should forgive people who sin against us seventy times seven! I do not think we need to keep track of how many times we need to forgive others. We should forgive and keep on forgiving. People do not get away with the wrongs they commit. Release them to the Lord and let God deal with them. Forgiveness unhooks you from the enemy and gives you freedom!

Then if my people who are called by my name will humble themselves and pray and seek my face and turn from their wicked ways, I will hear from heaven and will forgive their sins and restore their land.

2 Chronicles 7:14 NLT

We are God's people; He is talking to us. If we humble ourselves, seek His face, and do no more wicked things, God will hear and forgive us of our sins and restore our land. Praise Jesus! We humble ourselves, turn from sin now, and turn to you. Thank you for forgiving us and restoring us in Jesus' name. Repentance is a gift from God. Repentance is turning your face from sin and turning it back towards God, and sinning no more. "All those I dearly love I unmask and train. So, repent and be eager to pursue what is right." (Revelation 3:19 TPT). Submit to the training of the Lord and go after what is right. This is God's will for you. Righteousness and justice are the foundation of God's throne.

He Himself is the sacrifice that atones for our sins—and not only our sins but the sins of all the world.

1 John 2:2 NLT

Jesus is the sacrifice that atones for our sins and the sins of the world. His blood sacrifice was more than enough. We can't earn it. Jesus chose to do it for us before the foundation of the world. Thank you, Jesus, for sacrificing yourself for our freedom. We need to announce this to everyone. Jesus has paid the full price for the sins of the whole world. Salvation is only through Jesus. Everyone needs a Savior because we have all sinned and have fallen short of the glory of God.

The Power of Prayer

Are any of you suffering hardships? You should pray. Are any of you happy? You should sing praises. Are any of you sick? You should call for the elders of the church to come and pray over you, anointing you with oil in the name of the Lord. Such a prayer

offered in faith will heal the sick, and the Lord will make you well.
And if you have committed any sins, you will be forgiven. Confess
your sins to each other and pray for each other so that you may be
healed. The earnest prayer of a righteous person has great power
and produces wonderful results.

James 5:13-16 NLT

Here it tells us to be accountable and confess our sins to one another so we can be healed. Do you need to apologize to someone for anything you have done? Go and do it now so you may be healed. Do not be scared, because God is with you and in you. He will never leave you or forsake you. You never know what kind of restoration can come from this action of repentance. Jesus is the Restorer! We are to walk in the light as children of God. If, for some reason, you cannot go to the person, rest assured that confessing it to the Lord is taking care of it.

And whenever you stand praying, if you have anything against
anyone, forgive him and let it drop (leave it, let it go), in order that
your Father Who is in heaven may also forgive you your [own]
failings and shortcomings and let them drop. But if you do not

forgive, neither will your Father in heaven forgive your failings and

shortcomings.

Mark 11:25-26 AMPC

Here God is telling us to handle our business before we go into prayer. Release forgiveness to anyone you have a grudge against, so Father God will forgive you. It's written in red letters in the Bible, which means it's the words Jesus spoke. Be obedient to the Lord and release them now in Jesus' name. There's so much freedom in forgiving others and forgiving yourself. Verse 26 clearly says that if you do not forgive, your Father God will not forgive you. Thank the Lord that we can forgive by the power of the Holy Spirit within us. You don't have to do it alone. The Holy Spirit is waiting for you to release everyone to Him. You have to choose to forgive, and your feelings will follow. The decision or choice is yours. I pray you are willing to lay it down and surrender them to the Lord.

After meditating on these scriptures, I want you to close your eyes and lift your hands to the Lord. Whoever is coming to your mind of wrongs committed against you or your family, I want you to release them to the Lord right now. All you have to do is make the choice. Say 'Father God, I forgive this person and say their name. I release this person from all the wrongs committed against me and my family. I forgive him or her in Jesus' name. Forgiveness is a choice, and I choose to walk in love and forgiveness from here on out. Now, Holy Spirit, fill me up and deliver me from unforgiveness, bitterness, and offense, heal me in these areas of my soul right now in the name of Jesus. Heal my soul (mind, will, and emotions), my body, and my life where I was wounded by this sin of unforgiveness by the power of your Holy Spirit in Jesus' name. Amen'

I want you to do this prayer as many times as you need to, for as many people as you need to forgive. The Holy Spirit will be there with you in power to help you do this. We can't do it on our own, but through the power of the Holy Spirit, He will free us and heal us. Remember to forgive others and forgive yourself because Jesus has come and made a way for your forgiveness. It is finished. It is done. Do not wallow in a victim mentality, always thinking poor me, woe is me. This is stinking thinking and does not lead to life. Come out from that and receive all the good things the Lord has for you and your family. Receive it and walk in victory, paid for by the blood of Jesus in Jesus' name. The case in Heaven against you is closed. Keep it shut. Do not go back into sin. Look to Jesus to fill you in every area of your life. Invite Him in. We overcome because Jesus overcame! It's all rigged in our favor for victory!

6

Friend of God

Jesus said to him, "If you can believe,

all things are possible to him who believes."

Mark 9:23 NKJV

If you can believe all things are possible to you. With God all things are possible. You do not have to stay in a small place, stuck and bound by the devil. Jesus is the answer to all of your problems. You are a child of the Most High God, and freedom is yours today! Jesus is not hiding freedom from you. He is revealing Himself through the scriptures as you read this book, and the truth you receive will make you free. Yielding to the spirit of God and receiving revelation from the word of God will make you free. You are submitting to the authority and training of the Lord. When you submit to a greater authority, you walk in great authority. Jesus gave us authority to trample on serpents and scorpions. We crush the demons on our family bloodlines and allow freedom to flow in our lives and our families' lives. You are destined to take out your giant just like David did in the Bible. As you draw nearer to God, you will continue submitting to His authority, and the demons will listen to you because they will hear Jesus through you. They will flee from you. (James 4:7)

No longer do I call you servants, for a servant does not know what his master is doing; but I have called you friends, for all things that I heard from my father, I have made known to you.

John 15:15 NKJV

I remember where I was and what I was doing when God called me His friend. Often, the Lord will speak to me through a song. I was at our house in Arnaudville, La. I heard the song, Lean on Me, on the inside that I had not heard in many, many years.

It struck me in the heart, and I just knew in my knower that God was calling me His friend and that I could lean on Him for ALL of life's circumstances. You can call on the Lord 24/7. He is right there at every moment to hear and answer you. He's so good.

God is calling us His friends. And as His friend, He has revealed the mysteries of the Kingdom to us through His Word. As God reveals the mysteries of the Good News Gospel, and we understand them, we become Jesus's intimate friends. He is calling us to come up closer and higher to live a pure life of holiness and love. You will notice that you are becoming more and more like Jesus on your journey.

God's will is for you to be set apart for him in holiness and that you keep yourselves unpolluted from sexual defilement.

1 Thessalonians 4:3 TPT

For God's call on our lives is not to a life of compromise and perversion but to a life surrounded in holiness.

1 Thessalonians 4:7 TPT

Those who give thanks that Jesus is the Son of God live in God, and God lives in them. We have come into an intimate experience with God's love, and we trust in the love he has for us. God is love! Those who are living in love are living in God, and God lives through them.

1 John 4:15-16 TPT

For he has given us this command: whoever loves God must also demonstrate love to others.

1 John 4:21 TPT

Trust in the Lord with all your heart, And lean not on your own understanding; In all your ways acknowledge Him, And He shall direct your paths.

Proverbs 3:5-6 NKJV

The word "Trust" is defined in Webster's Dictionary (1828) as 1. Confidence: a reliance or resting of the mind on the integrity, veracity, justice, friendship, or other sound principle of another person. He that putteth his trust in the Lord shall be safe. (Proverbs 29:25)

God wants us to trust Him and know that we are safe in Him. Jesus is faithful and full of integrity. The foundation of God's throne is righteousness and justice. He wants us to be loyal so he can trust us. The Lord calls us to shut the door to all ungodliness and live a life set apart in purity, holiness, and righteousness. Jesus wants to have a very intimate relationship with us, for we are one, as John 17 says. As you spend time with the Lord, you will trust Him more because He will show Himself faithful to you. He will answer your questions and prayers. He is the one who directs our paths as we acknowledge Him in all our ways. He will lead and guide you through life's ups and downs. The Holy Spirit will never leave you or forsake you.

That they all may be one, [just] as You, Father, are in Me and I in You, that they also may be one in Us, so that the world may believe and be convinced that You have sent Me. I have given to them the glory and honor which You have given Me, that they may be one [even] as We are one: I in them and You in Me, in order that they may become one and perfectly united, that the world may know and[definitely] recognize that You sent Me and that You have loved them [even] as You have loved Me.

John 17:21-23 AMPC

We must trust God in all things and surrender all to Him. We must ask Him for help, strength, and divine intervention. We have to turn ourselves over to Him. We must allow the holy fire to burn up wrong thinking, speaking, and circumstances. We must yield to the holy fire and rely on God. As you develop your friendship with God, you will receive more and more revelation and understanding, and implement them in your life. God will then trust you and give you more.

Remember, Mark 9:23 says all things are possible to him who believes. Lord, help our unbelief. We repent for unbelief. Help us, Lord. We cannot fail if we do not quit, for Jesus prayed for us! He is our High Priest who is interceding for us now at the right hand of our Father God.

I can do all things through Christ who strengthens me.

Philippians 4:13 NKJV

For although we live in the natural realm, we don't wage a military campaign employing human weapons, using manipulation to achieve our aims. Instead, our spiritual weapons are energized with divine power to effectively dismantle the defenses behind which people hide. We can demolish every deceptive fantasy that opposes God and break through every arrogant attitude that is raised up in defiance of the true knowledge of God. We capture, like prisoners of war, every <u>*thought*</u> *and insist that it bow in obedience to the Anointed One. Since we are armed with such dynamic weaponry, we stand ready to punish any trace of rebellion, as soon as you choose complete obedience.*

2 Corinthians 10:3-6 TPT

We must win the battle of the mind by renewing our minds with the word of God and casting down every thought that rises up against the knowledge of Christ. Win the war in your mind and get the war out of you, then you will take out your giant. You have the power to control your thought life. This takes work. Please don't lose hope, keep working at it. The more you work at taking back your mind, the better it gets. You will stop receiving every thought that comes in as if it were yours. You must pull down every thought that exalts itself above the knowledge of Christ. Replace it with the word of God. The more you focus on the Lord and His word, the more you will be able to discern rightly what is good and what is evil, what is right and what is wrong. You will walk in the authority given to you by the Lord Jesus Christ. That starts by getting a hold of your mind. It's your mind. It is not the enemies. So do not let the enemy control your thoughts and life. Stand up and use the word of God and the name of Jesus, and take back your life!

We must do our part and build ourselves up in our most holy faith by praying in the Spirit (Jude 1:20). We must also take every thought captive and bring it into the obedience of Christ. This is vital for your divine transformation. You must become an expert at casting down every thought and vain imagination that exalts itself against the knowledge of Christ. Take out the giant that has been harassing you in your mind, your home, your family, and your job. You can do all things through Christ. Jesus is the name above all names. There is power in the name of Jesus. There is power in the blood of Jesus. Submit to God, resist the devil, and he will flee from you (James 4:7). Let's pray right now. I command all tormenting thoughts and mind control to cease and go now and never return in the name of Jesus. The blood of Jesus is against you, harassing demons; go now in Jesus' name. I release peace to every reader now in the name of Jesus. Lord, I ask you to fill every reader up with your Spirit until their cup overflows in Jesus' name. Fill every void in them, Lord, in Jesus' name, Amen. Thank you, Lord, for doing it now in Jesus' name. Amen.

Seven Things God Hates

There are six evils God truly hates and a seventh that is an abomination to him: Putting others down while considering yourself superior, spreading lies and rumors, spilling the blood of the innocent, plotting evil in your heart toward another, gloating over doing what's plainly wrong, spouting lies in false testimony, and stirring up strife between friends. These are entirely despicable to God!

Proverbs 6:16-19 TPT

We must know what Father God likes and what He hates. God hates these seven things: proud looks, lying tongues, hands that shed innocent blood, a heart that devises wicked plans, feet that run to evil, false testimony, and people who stir up strife and sow discord between friends and family. If you are doing these things, make the simple course correction and repent. "Prove by the way you live that you have repented of your sins and turned to God." (Matthew 3:8 NLT) The Lord will rise up in you to help you make the right choices. As you live continually in God's presence, living for Him becomes your passion. It becomes your greatest desire. Making the correct choices becomes clear to you. Remember, we always have a choice. It's up to us to choose right from wrong, good from evil, just from unjust. We need to accept the word of God as the absolute truth. It takes work, and we must do our part. We have a victory through Christ! Let the Lord burn up the chaff of ungodliness. Let the holy fire burn up all your wrong thinking and heal you now!! Do not delay!! Say, "Yes, Lord." Say, "Help me, Lord." Tell Jesus that, "I can't do anything without You! I need you every moment of every day."

Do not copy the behavior and customs of this world, but let God transform you into a new person by changing the way you think. Then you will learn to know God's will for you, which is good and pleasing and perfect.

Romans 12:2 NLT

And now, dear brothers and sisters, one final thing. Fix your thoughts on what is true, and honorable, and right, and pure, and lovely, and admirable. Think about things that are excellent and worthy of praise. Keep putting into practice all you learned and received from me—everything you heard from me and saw me doing. Then the God of peace will be with you.

Philippians 4:8-9 NLT

I have a testimony of winning the battle of the mind. The Lord personally taught me how to win the battle of the mind as a new Christian by going through the scriptures and then actually doing what they say to do. This helped me become free! Then, later, I participated in a book study with some ladies. The book's title was Power Thoughts. It was a 12-week book study on winning the battle of the mind. I had never read the book, but God had taken me through it in the Bible! The book study confirmed everything that the Holy Spirit taught me!! The Holy Spirit is such a great teacher!! My friend, Candy, and I also encouraged each other along the way! We need good friends in the Lord to encourage, sharpen one another, help each other, hold each other accountable, and persevere together. Ask God to send you on fire for God friends and get connected! Iron sharpens iron! (Proverbs 27:17) Find a bible believing church and put down roots. Find community and family. We are running our race together! My daughter said they have battle buddies in the National Guard! Get yourself a battle buddy in the Lord! We are made to be in unity to be one with each other in the Lord. (Ephesians 4:1-6, 1 Peter 3:8, Psalms 133:1) We all need ON FIRE FOR GOD FRIENDS!

We know our position by what Jesus did on the cross. And we know our identity in Christ…We are sons & daughters of the most high God, and we are seated together in heavenly places in him!

As I said, the Lord is calling us to draw closer and higher, to live a pure life of holiness and love. Tell God right now that you want the absolute truth, no matter what! Say, "God, I do not want to live in darkness, believing lies! Just give it to me straight, Lord, I can handle all things through you!"

We are not to walk on the fence with one foot in the world and one foot in the church. We are not to be lukewarm. (Revelation 3:15) We are to come out from the world and be separate. Set apart for God's glory. Transformation takes work, and God makes us better than we would be if things had never happened; that is how good He is. Hallelujah! Hallelujah to the Lamb! Thank you, Jesus! If God reveals it, He will heal it! We must be set apart and holy to fulfill our God given destinies.

Now, may the God of peace and harmony set you apart, making you completely holy. And may your entire being—spirit, soul, and body—be kept completely flawless in the appearing of our Lord Jesus, the Anointed One. The One who calls you by name is trustworthy and will thoroughly complete his work in you.

1 Thessalonians 5:23-24 TPT

Allow God to reveal His word to you, and it will make you free. Receive your deliverance as you allow God's truth inside of you to replace every lie. All the giants in your life must come down as you submit to the authority of Jesus in every area of your life. Drive out demons and forbid them to come back in Jesus' name. Don't give the devil another inch. The kingdom of God is continually expanding. Take back all the territory in your soul and then take back the territory everywhere you go: your home, place of work, business, school, etc. Meditate on these scriptures below. Receive the revelation of the power of the resurrection flowing through Jesus. It is the same power that raised Jesus from the dead. The Holy Spirit is the spirit of God. He is the resurrection power that lives inside of you, too.

A Boy Is Healed

And when He came to the disciples, He saw a great multitude around them, and scribes disputing with them. Immediately, when they saw Him, all the people were greatly amazed, and running to Him, greeted Him. And He asked the scribes, "What are you discussing with them?" Then one of the crowd answered and said, "Teacher, I brought You my son, who has a mute spirit. And wherever it seizes him, it throws him down; he foams at the mouth, gnashes his teeth, and becomes rigid. So I spoke to Your disciples, that they should cast it out, but they could not." He answered him and said, "O faithless generation, how long shall I be with you? How long shall I bear with you? Bring him to Me."

Then they brought him to Him. And when he saw Him, immediately the spirit convulsed him, and he fell on the ground and wallowed, foaming at the mouth. So He asked his father, "How long has this been happening to him?" And he said, "From childhood. And often he has thrown him both into the fire and into the water to destroy him. But if You can do anything, have compassion on us and help us." Jesus said to him, "If you can believe, all things are possible to him who believes." Immediately, the father of the child cried out and said with tears, "Lord, I believe; help my unbelief!" When Jesus saw that the people came running together, He rebuked the unclean spirit, saying to it: "Deaf and dumb spirit, I command you, come out of him and enter him no more!" Then the spirit cried out, convulsed him greatly, and came out of him. And he became as one dead, so that many said, "He is dead." But Jesus took him by the hand and lifted him up, and he arose. And when He had come into the house, His disciples asked Him privately, "Why could we not cast it out?" So He said to them, "This kind can come out by nothing but prayer and fasting."

Mark 9:14-29 NKJV

Then the seventy returned with joy, saying, "Lord, even the demons are subject to us in Your name." And He said to them, "I saw Satan fall like lightning from heaven. Behold, I give you the authority to trample on serpents and scorpions, and over all the power of the enemy, and nothing shall by any means hurt you. Nevertheless, do not rejoice in this, that the spirits are subject to you, but rather rejoice because your names are written in heaven."

Luke 10:17-20 NKJV

Mark 9 discusses how some spirits don't come out except through prayer and fasting. Prayer and fasting are a lifestyle that every Christian who walks in the supernatural power of God lives. It's a denial of yourself. Pushing the plate away and social media and TV to seek the Lord. Emptying yourself of selfish desires and your way, and seeking to know and experience the one true living God. More healing and freedom will come to you as you desire to know the truth and the Lord more.

Jesus saw satan fall like lightning from Heaven to Earth. Then He told us that He gives us authority over serpents and scorpions and over all the power of the enemy, and nothing will hurt us. So God gave you authority over the enemy harassing you. God is your fortress and hiding place (Psalms 91). In Him is all the power and authority you need to walk in freedom. I like to call it staying in my

'God Bubble' because I am safe in Him. This is where I am at peace and full of joy. You must learn to lean into the Lord and practice staying in His presence. The enemy will not want to be around you anymore as you walk closer and closer with the Lord.

God is around you, God is in you, and God is upon you! We have the best of both the Old and New Testaments because of Jesus' shed blood; we have the new covenant. In the Old Testament, God came upon the kings, priests, and prophets. In the New Testament, God is in the believer, and He comes upon us as well. God is calling you to Himself. Are you ready to take a stand? What's hindering you? Is it rejection, addiction, fear, anxiety, offenses, or unforgiveness? Are you busy and distracted? Are you prideful and always worried about yourself? If you are done with all addictions, rejection, fear, trauma, shame, offenses, anxiety, all distractions, and guilt, repent of it and renounce all evil now. You are royalty, and you are better than any of these things. So, say it with me, "I am Royalty, and I am better than that." The antidote to all of this is Jesus! Jesus is the answer to all of your problems. Pray aloud with me now, I repent and renounce all addictions, rejection, fear, trauma, shame, perversion, idolatry, guilt, grief, occult, wicca, witchcraft, rebellion, pride, religious spirit, poverty, narcissistic mindsets, gluttony, and anything else that's evil in me in Jesus' name. I command all you evil spirits to let go of this reader now and go and never return in Jesus' name. The blood of Jesus is against you, satan. I sever all evil spirits at the root in Jesus' name. You are permanently free. Whom the Son sets free is free indeed. Holy Spirit, fill this reader to overflowing and fill every void in them. There is no place left for the devil or his demons. Be filled continually with the Fire and Love of God in Jesus' name. Be healed and whole in every area of your life by the power of the Holy Spirit right now in Jesus' name. Amen.

You saw who you created me to be before I became me! Before I'd ever seen the light of day, the number of days you planned for me were already recorded in your book.

Psalms 139:16 TPT

Hallelujah. God wrote a beautiful book about you, as it says in Psalm 139:16. Pray with me now, Lord, I want to fulfill every page written in my book in Heaven! I want to live by the leading and the power of the Holy Spirit! Lord, reveal what you wrote in my book in Heaven. In Jesus' Name. Amen.

So now the case is closed. There remains no accusing voice of condemnation against those who are joined in life-union with Jesus, the Anointed One. For the "law" of the Spirit of life flowing through the anointing of Jesus has liberated us from the "law" of

sin and death. For God achieved what the law was unable to

accomplish because the law was limited by the weakness of

human nature. Yet God sent us his Son in human form to identify

with human weakness. Clothed with humanity, God's Son gave his

body to be the sin-offering so that God could once and for all

condemn the guilt and power of sin. So now every righteous

requirement of the law can be fulfilled through the Anointed One

living his life in us. And we are free to live, not according to our

flesh, but by the dynamic power of the Holy Spirit!

Romans 8:1-4 TPT

We must live from Romans 8, walking in the spirit and in freedom, not in condemnation. Remember, you were redeemed, and your sins are forgiven. God has removed them as far as the East is from the West. So, forgive yourself, get over yourself, and immerse yourself in the Lord! God wants to live His life in you and through you!

Do not be pulled into satan's ring of arguing, belittling, and gossiping. It does no good to get pulled into his ring because that is where he wins. Don't let satan steal your joy. If satan can get you to be offended, he has you oppressed and stuck right where he wants you. We must stay hidden in the Lord where we walk in VICTORY! In the shelter of the Most High God is where we belong! There the

Lord protects, heals, delivers, strengthens, and gives you Shalom in every area of your life. Shalom means more than peace; it also means nothing missing and nothing broken! Pray with me, Father God, in Jesus' name, we want Shalom in every area of our lives! We want healing, wholeness, prosperity, peace, and joy with You, Lord!

How God anointed and consecrated Jesus of Nazareth with the [Holy] Spirit and with strength and ability and power; how He went about doing good and, in particular, curing all who were harassed and oppressed by [the power of] the devil, for God was with Him.

Acts 10:38 AMPC

Then He said to His disciples, "The harvest is [indeed] plentiful, but the workers are few. So, pray to the Lord of the harvest to send out workers into His harvest."

Matthew 9:37-38 AMP

We are His workers! We must share the good news of the gospel with the people around us. God sent Jesus, and Jesus has sent us out to walk and do what He did. Jesus said that we would do even greater works than He did. So, yield to the supernatural power of God within you, and go about doing good and healing everyone who is harassed and oppressed by the devil. This is the will of God! We must walk in love and show compassion to others. Every day, the Lord sends us out. We are not alone on the mission! Whether you go to work or school, this is your mission field. This is your ministry. You were born and strategically placed in your area to help those around you. As you go, heal the sick, raise the dead, cleanse the lepers. Freely you have received and freely we are to give to others God puts in our path. Do good to those less fortunate than you. Do something nice for someone who can't pay you back. Take care of the widows and orphans around you. Be a servant. Lead by example. This is the culture of true Christianity. Deny yourself, take up your cross, and follow Jesus. Be a true disciple of Jesus Christ by living what the Word of God teaches you.

For I, the Lord your God, will hold your right hand, Saying to you, 'Fear not, I will help you.'

Isaiah 41:13 NKJV

God gives us orders. He prompts us to pray and do things for others in our path. Obedience is so important. Your obedience matters. It affects others around you. Don't be afraid because the Lord will help you. He is faithful. You are not alone because God is with you every step of the way. You can rely on the Holy Spirit.

You can see the people are sad, busted up, depressed, oppressed, and on the highway to hell. He sends us out to help them. Smile and share the love of Jesus. Share the truth with someone. The Lord will always be there to back you up. You will know when the Lord is telling you to speak to someone. Just do it! It may be a seed that you plant, or it may be their divine appointment to enter into the kingdom of Heaven!! This is so special, and when someone receives the Lord, all of Heaven rejoices! Hallelujah!!

Tell the devil where to go! Tell him you are in authority here, that you have the blood and name of Jesus, and that you will never stop using them. Keep him on the run! Give the devil a black eye! Keep him on the run! Pray in the Spirit throughout the day every day! Make the devil sorry he ever thought about touching you or your family or your finances in Jesus' name. We are Warriors in the Army of the Lord Jesus, and we do not back down, and we do not quit in Jesus' name! We never take off our armor! (Ephesians 6) Keep drawing near to God, and He will draw near to you. God rewards those who diligently seek Him! What are you waiting for? Set aside a specific time each day, especially for sitting and talking with God. Don't delay! Seek the Lord with your whole heart! Spending time with the Lord will help you to grow and mature. You will defeat every giant! We overcome because Jesus overcame! You are a friend of God! Make the Holy Spirit your best friend. You are one with God!

7

Victorious Living

The Lord your God is in your midst, A Warrior who saves.

He will rejoice over you with joy; He will be quiet in His love

[making no mention of your past sins],

He will rejoice over you with shouts of joy.

Zephaniah 3:17 AMP

Are you ready to be the church? Are you prepared to be the hands and feet of Jesus? Do you want to put your love into action?

If not now, when? My motto is "The church has left the building!" This new divine life you have in the Lord is to be cherished and shared with others. You are a warrior in the army of the Lord Jesus Christ. You are royalty. You have a God-given purpose, and one of them is that we have all been called to the ministry of reconciling people back to God. We all came from Him, and because of the fall, people need to hear the good news and be reconciled back to God. The Bible tells us to live as Jesus did by loving God, loving people, and making disciples.

Beloved friends, what should be our proper response to God's marvelous mercies? To surrender yourselves to God to be his sacred, living sacrifices. And live in holiness, experiencing all that delights his heart, for this becomes your genuine expression of worship.

Romans 12:1 TPT

Whether you eat or drink, live your life in a way that glorifies and honors God.

1 Corinthians 10:31 TPT

Living victoriously involves utilizing all the keys that have been revealed to you. Present your life as worship unto the Lord. Give Him your entire self and life by letting Him live through you. Honor and glorify Him in everything you do. Be the best spouse, mother or father, sister or brother, boss or employee, friend, disciple, and minister that you can be. Love like Jesus and continue building your relationship with the Lord and with other believers. Pray, fast, and meditate on the word of God. Become the warrior God created you to be! Get enrolled in Warrior Notes School of Ministry. Connect with a vibrant community of believers passionate about God. The Bible says, Iron sharpens Iron. Go out and be the hands and feet of Jesus in whatever way the Lord has gifted you to do. Do not sit on the bench or sidelines. Get into the game and do your part. Jesus is coming soon. Step out of the boat. Jesus is calling you to walk on water. He will be right there to back you up because He has sent you to minister to people. The Holy Spirit will show up in power, and people will be delivered, healed, and saved. Be joyful, willing, and obedient to the Lord! The Kingdom of God is always advancing, and we should be too. Everywhere you step, you are taking territory for the Lord. Neutral is not an option. If you are in neutral, you are really going backward and losing territory. Remember, Romans 8 is the template for your spiritual life. Meditate on it, and God will manifest it in you and through you. You will walk in power and victory in Christ!

And God has made all things new and reconciled us to himself, and given us the ministry of reconciling others to God. In other words, it was through the Anointed One that God was shepherding the world —not even keeping records of their transgressions —and he has entrusted to us the ministry of opening the door of reconciliation to God. We are ambassadors of the Anointed One who carry the message of Christ to the world, as though God were tenderly pleading with them directly through our lips. So, we tenderly plead with you on Christ's behalf, "Turn back to God and be reconciled to him." For God made the only one who did not know sin to become sin for us, so that we might become the righteousness of God through our union with him.

2 Corinthians 5:18-21 TPT

Then Jesus came close to them and said, "All authority of the universe has been given to me. Now wherever you go, make disciples of all nations, baptizing them in the name of the Father, the Son, and the Holy Spirit. And teach them to faithfully follow all that I have commanded you. And never forget that I am with you every day, even to the completion of this age."

Matthew 28:18-20 TPT

The Commission

And He said to them, 'Go into all the world and preach the gospel to every creature. He who believes and is baptized will be saved; but he who does not believe will be condemned. And these signs will follow those who believe: In My name they will cast out demons; they will speak with new tongues; they will take up serpents; and if they drink anything deadly, it will by no means hurt them; they will lay hands on the sick, and they will recover."

Mark 16:15-18 NKJV

Victorious believers walk in the Spirit and are led by the Holy Spirit in all they do. The fruit of the Spirit is love, joy, peace, long-suffering, kindness, goodness, faithfulness, gentleness, and self-control. Living life victoriously comes from our intimate relationship with Jesus. Our life is an outflow of living in the secret place. We are in a beautiful partnership with God when we delight ourselves in Him and surrender all to him. Our hearts are on fire and burn with passion for the one true living God. We must share our love for Jesus with others by showing compassion for people and by reaching out to those in need — widows, orphans, the elderly, the homeless, single parents, and children. We must share our testimonies. We overcome by blood of the Lamb and the word of our testimony. (Rev. 12:11)

Victorious Believers love, honor, and serve Jesus, and His people; we worship and glorify the Most High God; we make our lives a prayer; and are in unity with God and each other. Victorious Believers seek first the kingdom of God and His righteousness. We share the truth in love. We walk in humility, forgiveness, and daily repentance. Pray compassionately for one another. We worship Jesus, the King of Kings. We love everyone. We are ambassadors for Christ Jesus. He has given us the Ministry of Reconciliation and the command to go and make disciples. We are fishers of men. Pointing people to Jesus, who is The Way, The Truth, and The Life.

Victorious Believers do their God-given part. Each one of us has special gifts and talents from God, and we all work together to complete the Lord's mission. Jesus is the only Door to the Father, the one true living God, who came in the flesh, died on the cross, rose on the third day, and ascended into Heaven. Whose body was broken and whose blood was shed in love, so we could be forgiven, set free, healed, redeemed, and have prosperous everlasting life! Shalom! Victorious Believers will baptize people in water, in the Holy Spirit, and in Fire. We will pray in tongues and use the gifts of the Holy Spirit to edify and build each other up. We will walk in holiness and in the fear of the Lord and teach others to do the same. We are the move of God in our homes, communities, and in the nations.

We are the hands and feet of Jesus, helping to bring in the end-time harvest of souls. We will walk in the supernatural power of God. As we go, we will preach that the kingdom of God is at hand to heal the sick, cleanse the lepers, raise the dead, and cast out demons. Miracles, signs, and wonders shall follow us (believing ones) as we preach, teach, and demonstrate the Good News Gospel. We are committed to helping widows, orphans, the elderly, single parents, children, and others in need. We are blessed to be a blessing. Freely we have received, and freely we give. We train up Warriors and pass the torch to the younger generations. We love and value our youth. We will lead by example, living our lives with biblical morals and values. (Galatians 5) We take care of our families, including our parents and grandparents. We walk by faith and trust the Lord. We carry out the Lord's divine purposes and plans He wrote in our books in Heaven. May everything we do be done in love, obedience, and worship to our Father God until Jesus returns. Shalom!

A warrior after God's heart is a man of true integrity. He lays his life down for others. A warrior after God's heart rises and doesn't back down from a challenge. He makes a stand for truth, justice, and righteousness. He is walking in the peace of God, wearing the whole armor of God, and defended by the Word of God. A true warrior knows his authority in Christ Jesus and fights against every evil thing: the devil, the world, and self. A warrior is always obedient to his commander.

We are warriors. We love God and people. Warriors lead by serving well and having compassion for others, for it is more blessed to give than to receive. True Warriors live out the Gospel every day. Cultivate a community of believers where people are loved, safe, & have value. This is what everyone needs.

The Community of Believers

Every believer was faithfully devoted to following the teachings of the apostles. Their hearts were mutually linked, sharing communion and coming together regularly for prayer. A deep sense of holy awe swept over everyone, and the apostles performed many miraculous signs and wonders. All the believers were in fellowship as one body, and they shared with one another whatever they had. Out of generosity, they even sold their assets to distribute the proceeds to those who were in need among them. Daily, they met together in the temple courts and in one another's homes to celebrate communion. They shared meals together with joyful hearts and tender humility. They were continually filled with praises to God, enjoying the favor of all the people. And the Lord kept adding to their number daily those who were coming to life.

Acts 2:42-47 TPT

"A new commandment I give to you, that you love one another; as I have loved you, that you also love one another. By this all will know that you are My disciples, if you have love for one another."

John 13:34-35 NKJV

Jesus said: "and said to them, 'Come follow me and I will transform you into fishers of men instead of fish!"

Mark 1:17 TPT

Testimony, I was praying with my eyes closed, and I asked God what He wanted me to do. God had me look down and open my eyes there on my arm, and in big white letters I saw the word FISHING—I knew it in my knower that the Holy Spirit was telling me He wanted me to go fishing for men! I remember which shirt I was wearing that day- a HUK fishing shirt. I will never forget this. Living a life full of God Adventures is THE BEST LIFE EVER. I encourage you to do your part in the army of the Lord and live victoriously in this life while qualifying for your heavenly position. Grow closer to the Lord every day and become so in love with Him that you will do anything for Him. He desires to be so close to you. He loves you so much. You will not regret pursuing God. You will be full of joy and gratitude, and so full of His Holy Spirit. People will really wonder what happened to you. They will not recognize you, and they will want to know all about your divine transformation. You will be able to tell them about your supernatural-transforming God and how, through Him, you overcame —and that they can overcome too, just like you! You overcome by the blood of the lamb and the word of your testimony (Revelation 12:11).

Continue going after God! Be the hands and feet of Jesus! Be the Church! If not now, when? Make this your motto: 'THE CHURCH HAS LEFT THE BUILDING!'

Continue Jesus Mission

"The Spirit of the Lord is upon me, and he has anointed me to be hope for the poor (preach good news gospel), healing for the brokenhearted, and new eyes for the blind, and to preach to prisoners, 'You are set free!' I have come to share the message of

Jubilee, for the time of God's great acceptance has begun."

Luke 4:18-19 TPT

True spirituality that is pure in the eyes of our Father God is to make a difference in the lives of the orphans, and widows in their troubles, and to refuse to be corrupted by the world's values.

James (Jacob) 1:27 TPT

"And as you go, preach, saying, 'The kingdom of heaven is at hand.' Heal the sick, cleanse the lepers, raise the dead, cast out demons. Freely you have received, freely give."

Matthew 10:7-8 NKJV

Men of Israel, hear these words: Jesus of Nazareth, a Man attested by God to you by miracles, wonders, and signs which God did through Him in your midst, as you yourselves also know—

Acts 2:22 NKJV

Then He said to His disciples, "The harvest truly is plentiful, but the laborers are few. Therefore, pray the Lord of the harvest to send out laborers into His harvest."

Matthew 9:37-38 NKJV

Victorious Warriors are on a mission to glorify God, to reconcile people to God, to make disciples, to help those in need, and to walk in unity and love, fulfilling every page written in our books in Heaven until Jesus returns.

I pray for everyone who reads this book:

Father God, I ask you in Jesus' name to bless every reader with eyes to see you and ears to hear you. I break the power of satan over every reader now in Jesus' name. I pray that you may daily receive wisdom, revelation, and understanding from the Lord as you seek Him and meditate on the Word of God. I pray you will fulfill every page written in your books in Heaven. I activate the gifts and callings in you, and I command them to come forth now. I pray that you yield to the Holy Fire and allow God to burn up everything that is not of God, and you come out purified like gold and will walk in the Fire of God. I pray for you to have an intimate and beautiful relationship with the Lord. I pray that you may have continual habitation with the Lord and receive more revelations and visitations. I pray you will do your part to help bring in the great harvest of souls. I pray for you and for your family to love and serve the Lord all the days of your lives. I pray for Shalom to come to every area of your life and for fruit that remains in Jesus' name. Amen!

References

"Acceleration" Definition of acceleration from the Cambridge

    Advanced Learner's Dictionary & Thesaurus © Cambridge

    University Press.

"Advocate." Merriam-Webster.com Dictionary, Merriam-Webster,

    https://www.merriam-webster.com/dictionary/advocate.

    Accessed 2 Aug. 2024.

Amplified® Bible, The Lockman Foundation, La Habra, CA 90631,

    Copyright ©2015, All rights reserved.

http://www.lockman.org

Amplified Bible Classic Edition, The Lockman Foundation, La Habra,

    CA 90631, Copyright 1954, 1958, 1962, 1964, 1965, 1987, All

    rights reserved. http://www.lockman.org.

"Change." Webster Dictionary 1828 - Webster's Dictionary 1828 –

    Change

    https://webstersdictionary1828.com/Dictionary/change.

    Accessed August 10, 2024.

"Comforter." Merriam-Webster.com Dictionary, Merriam-Webster,

https://www.merriam-webster.com/dictionary/comforter.
Accessed 2 Aug. 2024.

"Counselor." Merriam-Webster.com Dictionary, Merriam-Webster,

https://www.merriam-webster.com/dictionary/counselor.
Accessed 21 Oct. 2025.

"Divine." Webster Dictionary 1828 - Webster's Dictionary 1828 –

Divine
https://webstersdictionary1828.com/Dictionary/divine.
Accessed August 10, 2024.

"Forgiven." Merriam-Webster.com Thesaurus, Merriam-Webster,

https://www.merriam-webster.com/thesaurus/forgiven.
Accessed 3 Aug. 2024.

"Holy." Merriam-Webster.com Dictionary, Merriam-Webster,

https://www.merriam-webster.com/dictionary/holy.
Accessed 2 Aug. 2024.

The Holy Bible, New King James Version, Thomas Nelson, Copyright

© 1982 All rights reserved.

Holy Bible, New Living Translation, copyright © 1996, 2004, 2015 by

"Standby." Merriam-Webster.com Dictionary, Merriam-Webster,

https://www.merriam-webster.com/dictionary/standby. Accessed 2 Aug. 2024.

"Transformation." Webster Dictionary 1828 - Webster's Dictionary

1828Transformation.https://webstersdictionary1828.com/Dictionary/ transformation. Accessed August 10, 2024.

"Trust." Webster Dictionary 1828 - Webster's Dictionary 1828 - Trust.

Accessed https://webstersdictionary1828.com/Dictionary/trust August 10, 2024.

About the Author

Dr. Rachel Comeaux is a Pastor at Warrior Fellowship of Lafayette whose life is a testimony to God's transforming grace. After walking through deep personal trials and healing, she was called into ministry at age 38, earned her doctoral degree in Bible and Theology through Warrior Notes School of Ministry, and now helps others experience freedom and lasting change alongside her husband, Shep, in Lafayette, La. They are a blended family with five beautiful children.

Notes: